Becoming A Powerful Christian

7 Secrets to a Life of Miracles and Answered Prayer

By
Marjorie Lou

Unless otherwise indicated, all Scripture quotations are from The Holy Bible, English Standard Version® (ESV®), copyright © 2001 by Crossway, a publishing ministry of Good News Publishers. Used by permission. All rights reserved.

Becoming a Powerful Christian
ISBN: 978-1-947624-04-7 Paperback Edition
ISBN: 978-1-947624-02-3 eBook .mobi for Kindle Edition
ISBN: 978-1-947624-03-0 eBook epub Edition
ISBN: 978-1-947624-05-4 Audio Book Edition
ISBN: 978-1-947624-06-1 Hard Cover Edition

Publisher
Marjorie Lou Ministries
PO Box 75
Seville, FL 32190
Marjorielou.com

Cover Designer
Marchon Lagapa Pulido

Copyright © 2018 by Marjorie Lou Ministries

Printed in the United States of America. All rights reserved under International Copyright law. No part of this publication may be reproduced, distributed, or transmitted in any form or by any means, including photocopying, recording, or other electronic or mechanical methods, without the prior written permission of the publisher, except in the case of brief quotations embodied in reviews and certain other non-commercial uses permitted by copyright law.

TABLE OF CONTENTS

Introduction 7

Chapter 1 The Problem Today 11

Chapter 2 Why You Need God's Power 15

Chapter 3 What is This Power 29

Chapter 4 Secret One – The Power Source 41

Chapter 5 Secret Two – Keep Your Keys in Your Pocket .. 55

Chapter 6 Secret Three – A Common Thread 65

Chapter 7 Secret Four – Get in the Word 81

Chapter 8 Secret Five – The Spoken Word 107

Chapter 9 Secret Six – The Power of Believing 129

Chapter 10 Secret Seven – Authority 141

Chapter 11 Powerful Christians Pray It Out 153

Chapter 12 Powerful Christians Live It Out 177

Chapter 13 The Valley of Decision 191

DOWNLOAD THE AUDIO BOOK FREE!

Read This First

As a special thank you for buying this book I would like to give you the Audio Book Edition

100% FREE

To Download Go To:

MarjorieLou.com/powerful-Christian-audiobook

INTRODUCTION

The Bible is full of examples of Christians walking in the power of God. The Great Commission as recorded in Mark tells us signs of God's power follow believers and it tells us God does this to confirm that what the believer is saying is really from Him. Jesus Himself described how He expected believers to walk in God's power. Few Christians today look anything like the believers Jesus described. Jesus commanded believers to heal the sick, cast out demons, and raise the dead. Are you a believer with these kinds of signs following you? Instead of experiencing God's power, you are frustrated that your prayers never seem to really be answered, perplexed why miracles only happen for other people, and do not see Bible promises coming true in your life.

This book tells you how to be that Christian who taps into God's power, prays prayers that get answered, and changes the world around them. *Becoming A Powerful Christian* is designed to resolve the problem of why God's power is foreign to you and teaches why God earnestly desires for you to use His power. This book reveals secrets of God's power plainly taught in the Bible, readily taught in the early church, but rarely taught in churches today.

I was a weak powerless Christian, determined to find the answer to why only a few people knew God's power in their lives. What was the secret? Did it require a certain level of spirituality? Was it for people who were good enough, read the Bible the most, or prayed longer than others?

With the promise of "seek and you shall find," I set out on a journey to find these answers. Turns out, God wanted me to know – needed me to know – the truth.

The answer shocked me. But what really took me by surprise is that rarely were these truths being taught in churches.

Having spent over thirteen years walking in God's power and teaching this amazing truth to others, I have seen tremendous miracles. Every member of my household experiences God's power, and many regular people (just like me) also begin walking in the power once they learned the secrets in the Bible I will show you in this book.

Many who have learned these secrets about God's power now experience that power in everyday life. They and their families are no longer victims of fate, but now respond to circumstances in life with God's perspective, living a life of miracles and answered prayers, enabling them to help others as well. This is exactly how Jesus lived, serving others through the power of God. Jesus said you would do greater things than He did, and you will once you understand scriptures pertaining to God's power.

After teaching my preteen daughter the secrets I will reveal in this book, she laid hands on a church leader who was having chronic back issues. The back pains left immediately, and three days later the leader reported that the pains never returned; however, a good night's sleep had returned for the first time in months. The church leader gave the testimony about my daughter and the video of this testimony is one of my prized possessions, because it is a testimony to the reality of the power of God working through an ordinary person who simply understood and believed what scripture teaches.

Like the everyday people I have taught in my seminars, once you understand God's Word as it pertains to His power, you too will:

> pray prayers that get answered,
>
> lay hands on the sick and they recover,
>
> break the chains of emotions that control you, setting you free to live the peaceful, powerful life Jesus promised you,
>
> see God's blessings and provision for your family,
>
> cast demons out of your life and out of your home, utilizing the fullness of God's protection over your household,

and you can do it without passing a test of being good enough or spiritual enough.

It took me decades to find answers to questions that I should have learned from the beginning. I wasted years of my life frustrated that I could not seem to live the way Jesus wanted me to, even though I tried and desired to do what is right. Do not spend one more minute of your life struggling with every scheme the devil throws at you. Your answers are in this book. God made His power available so that you can enjoy the provision and protection He promises you. God wants you equipped to accomplish the tasks He has set before you. Don't miss your opportunity to hear God say to you, "Well done good and faithful servant" simply because you did not take this opportunity to learn how to tap into His power.

I am about to unlock the secrets to grabbing hold of and tapping into God's power in your life. All you must do to experience this power is to keep reading. Make sure you do not skip any chapters, for each chapter lays the groundwork for understanding the subsequent chapters. Once you reach the end of this book, you will be educated, equipped and already starting to experience God's power in your life. Are you ready to begin your life of miracles and answered prayers? Then turn the page and let's get started!

Chapter 1

The Problem Today

I love the church! It is powerful and glorious, revealing the majesty of its creator and bridegroom, Jesus Christ. The church was born in the power of God on the day of Pentecost and continued in power by the Holy Spirit throughout its early days. Anywhere the gospel was taken, miracles happened, signs and wonders prevailed, societies were disrupted, and entire towns were changed.

Throughout history, anywhere you find the church in its pure form, you see the power of God holding it, protecting it, providing for it, and sending it forth to do the impossible to reach the lost for Christ. It is the power of God that keeps it alive, still functioning 2,000 years after inception, surviving persecution at every turn.

God designed the church so that each member becomes a crucial element of her, each being relied on by the others to fulfill the specific destinies that God determined for them before the foundation of the world. God equips each believer with the power they need to accomplish the Kingdom work set before them. When each member fulfills their purpose, the Kingdom functions effectively to reach the world for the cause of Christ, perfectly orchestrated by God the Father. It is a marvelous supernatural performance that puts the enemy at bay and sets the captives free.

The Problem

Something has happened to the modern church. She has lost her vision of who she is, her understanding of what the Kingdom of God is, and her purpose in it. She no longer thirsts for the Word, which is her very nourishment. No more does she shake society, but to the contrary, gives way to the pressure of social and political agendas begging her to bow the knee to another god. The values of the church blanketed Western society for centuries, revealing itself in such ways as service to others, honesty, integrity and grit to stand up in the face of peril for what is pure and righteous and revered. Now these noble characteristics are slandered and ridiculed. Where is the stamina and the fortitude the church is renowned for in past centuries? What happened to her?

The church has lost her power. She began to slumber in the lazy days of blessing and is just now waking up to the realization that while her guard was down, something changed. The Bible became just a book, the Savior reduced to a mere ticket into a pearly gate, and church gatherings of service-minded saints became social clubs full of self-focused members quarreling over petty issues with little attention on the Kingdom of God or its purpose.

Without the power of God, the church has no purpose, no life, no means by which to function. Once the power is removed, the church becomes a lifeless man-made man-powered group no longer shaking the foundations of society but is itself being shaken and threatened until it conforms to the world's way of thinking and acting.

Without the power of God, the church has fallen to the attacks of Satan and is permeated by worldly thinking. It crept in through our altars and slithered down the aisles to the very pew where you sit. We took it home where it entered our families and relationships, implementing its war strategies of destruction against our marriages and the hearts of our children. With God's power foreign to us, we did not know how to fight back, because we did not know what we were battling against.

The Solution

It is time for those who name the name of Jesus Christ to rise up, shake a fist at the devil and shout, "No more in my house!"

Christians across this country are taking this stand and finding God's power and protection for their life and their family. These powerful Christians bring change wherever they go. Their families share bonded hearts. Their marriages grow strong. Their children influence other children for goodness and righteousness and grow up without falling away into the world's temptations.

This will become your life's story when you become a strong Christian living in God's power. Not only will your family reap tremendous benefits of peace in your home, but you will join the ranks of other powerful people living their lives to fulfill God's purpose. When Christians repent at the altar then take back God's power that He has made available to them, once again will the church disrupt society and bring this nation humbly to its knees before the true and living God.

Every Christian has a responsibility to God our Father. He loves us so much, He was willing to send His only Son to suffer and die to rescue us from sure destruction. If you name the name of Jesus Christ and believe upon Him for that salvation, you are called by Him to fulfill a destiny. You have a crucial part to play in human history and God is relying on you, His servant and His child, to accomplish what He is calling you do to, in your family and in your world. You will never accomplish any of it without the power of God.

The immeasurable greatness of God's power is available to you as a believer. But it is for one purpose – for you to fulfill your destiny in the Kingdom of God. If you and I would each say to God, "I am here Lord!" the church would once again be the light shining on a hill to this nation and this nation would once again be a beacon of light for all the world to see.

Before we jump into the lost secrets of how to experience God's power in your life, let me show you the benefits for you and your family when you learn how to tap into all God has provided. You will be pleasantly surprised at what God has in store for you!

Chapter 2

Why You Need God's Power

Before discussing how to be powerful, I want to be sure you have a vision for why this issue is so critical. For some, the question lingers as to why, as a Christian, I should care. What's the big deal anyway? Isn't it enough if I attend church and live a clean life and teach my children how to know right from wrong? That power stuff may be great for others, but I don't expect to go out and perform miracles. That's the Pastor's job. Or maybe it is just for that guy I saw doing it on a television show.

I have identified six major reasons it is crucial for you as a Christian to know God's power and understand how to use it in your life.

Reason 1-A Witness

The power of God permeates the stories of the Old and New Testaments in the Bible. Each time God's power is revealed, people fall on their faces and worship the true and living God. God's power has a way of breaking through the veil of heaven and manifesting a physical proof that He is real and mighty.

Here are a few examples:

When Elijah faced Ahab concerning truth in God, he ordered a contest of sorts to prove whose God was real, the God of Abraham, Isaac and Jacob, or the god of Baal. The prophets of Baal were to cut a bull in pieces and put in on an altar with wood, but put no fire to it. If Baal were real, it would be up to Baal to bring the fire to consume the bull. Ahab's prophets cried out all day to this false god, yet nothing happened to the bull or the wood.

When it was time for God's prophet Elijah's turn to do the same, he ordered a bull be cut in pieces and placed on the altar. Then he had a trench build around the altar that would hold gallons of water. Next, he had water poured over the altar enough to drench the bull, the wood, and altar until it overflowed and filled the trench. Only then did he pray that God would bring fire to consume the bull.

Elijah had no need to cry out all day. With only a short prayer of faith, immediately fire fell and consumed the bull, the wood, the stones of the altar, the water around the altar, and the dust of the ground.

> *And when all the people saw it,*
> *they fell on their faces and said,*
> *"The Lord, he is God; the Lord, he is God."*
>
> *I Kings 18:39*

King Nebuchadnezzar had a dream that was troubling him, and he could no longer sleep at night. He ordered all his wise counselors to come and, not just interpret the dream, but also tell what the dream was in the first place. Since there were none who could, the king ordered all the wise men of Babylon to be killed. Daniel was one of the wise men, having been carried away from Israel in an invasion and made to serve the King in his administration. Daniel sought an appointment with the king, and when granted the meeting, told him both the dream and the interpretation.

> *Then King Nebuchadnezzar fell upon his face...*
> *The king answered and said to Daniel,*
> *"Truly your God is the God of gods*
> *and the Lord of kings."*
>
> Daniel 2:46-47

After the reign of King Nebuchadnezzar, Daniel continued to serve in the administration of subsequent kings. When King Darius reigned, evil and jealous men tried to get rid of Daniel by tricking the king into making a decree that, by penalty of death, no one in the kingdom could petition any other king or god except King Darius for a period of thirty days. They knew Daniel would pray to his God and could have him easily disposed of. As a man of faith, Daniel did not try to hide his prayers but opened his window and prayed three times daily just as he always had. When King Darius realized he had been tricked, he was grieved because he liked Daniel. His law was unchangeable, mainly because of the total humiliation he would face, since a change would be perceived as weakness. Daniel was thrown in a den of lions as his death sentence.

The next morning, when King Darius discovered that God sent an angel to shut the mouths of the lions and Daniel had not been harmed, he wrote:

> *"I make a decree in all my royal dominion people are to tremble and fear before the God of Daniel, for he is the living God, enduring forever; his kingdom shall never be destroyed, and his dominion shall be to the end. He delivers and rescues; he works signs and wonders in heaven and on earth, he who has saved Daniel from the power of the lions."*
>
> Daniel 6:26-27

When the truth of God's power is manifested before people, they have an opportunity to see the reality of the One True God. As a result, they fall on their faces and worship Him. Many people have been saved just because they saw similar manifestations of God's power, because it proves God is real, unhinges all the previous beliefs they had about Him, and opens their hearts to believe on Him.

Reason 2-The Kingdom

The second reason every Christian must experience God's power is because God has a kingdom. Like any governmental structure, there are many operations of His Kingdom that need to be carried out. Since God's Kingdom is a supernatural kingdom, the work to be done is supernatural as well. A major portion of the Kingdom work is carried out through humans. God works through humans who are willing to do what He has called them to do. God does not assign supernatural tasks and expect them fulfilled with human abilities. He equips believers with His abilities and every weapon in His arsenal, so they can get the job done efficiently and effectively.

What are some of these jobs?

- Taking the gospel to all the world
- Raising children within strong households, fortifying them in Jesus Christ so they can withstand all the pressures culture places on them
- Gathering in all the provisions God supplies
- Overcoming evil people who mean to do you harm
- Fighting Satan's attacks against your marriage, your children, or any other relationships in your life
- Fighting Satan's attacks against your body, or those of your household, your church, your neighborhood – attacks in the form of sickness, injury or disease
- Casting out the demonic forces that seek to kill, steal and destroy people in your sphere of influence
- Standing for the truth of Jesus Christ in your household, your neighborhood, your workplace, or the world, no matter what others deem politically correct

God is not asking you to consider doing these jobs. God knows that when you are married, you must rely on Him for that marriage to be successful. When you have children, you must rely on Him to prevent them from being swallowed up by an evil-prevalent culture. When you face sickness, you must rely on the only healer that brings true complete healing.

God does all these things with His power. But later in the book we will see that God does all these things with His power *working through human beings*. God is relying on you to pick up His weapons and get the job done. He expects you to know those weapons and use them for His purposes.

Why does He expect this? Because He wants you to have a successful marriage and strong children. He wants you to have a sound mind, and peace that surpasses all understanding. He wants you to know the fullness of His blessing and promises. He also wants His Kingdom work done.

When you have all these things, you have done great damage to the enemy's camp. His schemes fail, and his destruction halted. At the same time, you have accomplished glorious feats for your King. None of this can be accomplished without God's power flowing in your life.

Reason 3-Protection From the Enemy

It is not a pleasant thing to think about, but knowing the truth about the enemy will help you get your perspective straight and will drastically change what you deem important in your life. Satan loathes humans, hence the third reason you must experience the power of God in your life. Satan wants humans destroyed and has sent his minions with marching orders:

Kill your power, your relationships, your connection to God

Steal your joy, your peace, your effectiveness for God, and your trust in His Word.

Destroy the lives and bodies of every living human being on Earth

I consider this a real and present danger for you and your household. So, what do you do about it?

- You can stick your head in the sand and pretend it's not real.

- You can brush it off and hope everything turns out okay.
- You can worry, fret, and panic
- You can put all your human effort to dealing with this enemy.
- You can cry out to God for him to do something about it.
- Or you can recognize that God has done something about it and take up His sword to stop the enemy's work in your life.

God knows how He intends you to deal with it. He sent Jesus Christ to conquer the enemy and make a triumph over him. The work is done. Now when the enemy tries to come back at you, you have a weapon – God's very power.

Have you had opportunity to be around chickens? When a mother hen has a brood of babies, she has a special call she gives that only her babies know. The mom gives that call at any sign of danger, and the babies come running from everywhere straight under the wing of the mother. The mother spreads that wing and haunches down, providing an umbrella of protection for those babies. Any hawk who wants one of her babies will have to go through her to get them.

What happens to a chick who will not heed the voice of the mother hen? It is left vulnerable to the will of the hawk. There is nothing the mother will do to try and save that baby, because to do so puts the whole brood at risk. She has made a provision of protection, and it is up to each chick to trust her for safety.

God has given you an umbrella of protection called the shelter of the Most High God.[1] If you will heed His voice and run into the shelter, you will enjoy the safety and protection He provides for his own. His protection is perfect. Satan will never penetrate that barrier of protection. If you refuse to run in, you are left vulnerable to the will and ways of Satan. Human effort is outside God's shelter of protection. The only thing that is effective in God's kingdom is His way, His will, His power and His Word. It is just like the chick who must rely on mother hen's way. For it to rely on its own efforts means sure destruction from the hawk.

You may say it doesn't really matter for your life, thinking that you can handle this on your own. You are that chick outside the wing of protection. But it is not just you that is affected. Your spouse is affected. Your children are left vulnerable. You wonder why nothing seems to go your way and you feel like you are always being knocked down in life.

Your family depends on you to be strong and utilize all God provides. You must give up all the old ways that have been failing you and take up God's power, so you can enjoy the protection against this enemy that it provides for you and your family. Only God knows how to overcome Satan, and He has overcome him in Jesus Christ. Jesus paid a great price to put this power in your hands, and he expects you to use it to keep Satan at bay from your household, so he cannot hurt you or your family.

Reason 4-Social or Economic Breakdown

How often have you heard of the threat of an impending breakdown in our society? A decade ago, this was considered conspiracy talk. Today it has become so mainstream that there are reality shows on television about preparing for it.

I am not proposing whether impending crisis is a threat or not, but for the sake of prudency, consider what you would do if trouble reached our shores. If food and medical care became so extravagantly expensive – or simply disappeared – due to war, economic collapse or social breakdown, what will you do?

I write these words as an influenza epidemic is breaking out across our country killing thousands of otherwise strong and healthy people. Hospitals are overloaded, many resorting to setting up tents in parking lots to handle the influx of cases. I trust that by the time this book is in your hands, it will be an old story; however, should it continue to grow, you can be certain that man's resources will quickly diminish, and the hospitals will not be able to do much to care for the sick or stop it from spreading.

If you depend on the medical system for your needs, it will fail, as do all human efforts. Even in "normal" times, how often does the medical system give disappointing results? God never intended for humans to depend on man-made systems and solutions. We are to depend on God alone and He is more than able to take care of your every need, even in sickness. God's power is available to protect you and stop this enemy attack from touching your household. When your household is untouched in a time of trouble, people will notice and opportunities for the gospel will explode.

In a time of epidemic, when the church knows how to lay hands on the sick and they recover, people will flock to its doors because the power of Jesus Christ will be their only hope. As they come, the church will be able to give them hope for their souls as well as their bodies. In a time of economic crisis, the church may be the only means of food. As people flock to the churches for bread, they will also receive the bread of life.

Today, few seem interested in crossing the threshold of church buildings. Should we encounter desperate times in the future, people will be beating down the doors of those churches who know their God, all because of God's power flowing through believers who will take up that power and use it for His glory.

Reason 5-Your Family Depends on You

God instituted the family to be a picture of spiritual things. It is designed after heavenly patterns and truths and works correctly when the design specifications are properly met. Anything designed in human form will fail. Human methods and solutions always ultimately fail. When a family is structured by God's function and design, it will flourish and enjoy the love, peace, and joy it was meant to give.

Because the family is patterned after God's Kingdom, we see correlations in how the structure of the unit is built, utilizing levels of authority. (I discuss how authority works later in this book.) When each level on the chain of authority utilizes God's power, it builds a perfect dome over families for protection and provides love and peace within its walls.

With God's power instituted at every level, the home has nothing to fear. Relationships flourish, hearts bond, children train up in the way they should go, and every member of the household matures into higher levels in Christ. The whole unit functions as a team.

Outside that dome, the enemy lurks with an arsenal of schemes to destroy the family. But the enemy's attacks cannot penetrate a home full of God's power. When crisis comes, the powerful Christian family withstands the attack and sends the devil running. Sickness is healed, demons are cast out, and attacks against the minds of you, your spouse or your children are thwarted by other family members who recognize what is happening and step in quickly to resist it. The enemy is forced to retreat with its tail between its legs.

Reason 6-Your Destiny

You have a destiny determined before the foundation of the world and it is your job in this world to find it, follow it, and fulfill it. Nothing in this life will bring fulfillment and satisfaction as knowing you are walking in the calling God has placed on your life.

Be assured of this one thing: you will never stumble upon your calling. It will take determination on your part to find it and the power of God in your life to walk it out.

There is one thing I live for in my life and everything about my life is designed to meet this one goal. My goal is to hear these words:

> *His master said to him,*
> *"Well done, good and faithful servant.*
> *You have been faithful over a little;*
> *I will set you over much.*
> *Enter into the joy of your master."*
>
> *Matthew 25:21*

Nothing else matters to me but to hear Jesus say these words on the appointed day. My marriage, my parenting, my work, my relationships with others – I live out all these things with a Kingdom mindset doing all that Jesus has destined for me to do.

This is the reason I have spent so much time learning how to walk in the power of God, so that I am an able and yielded vessel ready to fulfill the calling God placed upon my life from the foundation of the world. Then one day I will hear, "Well done! Enter into the joy of your Master!" That is where I plan to spend eternity, in the joy of my Master.

The exceeding greatness of God will never be revealed to a hurt and dying world until believers dare to believe, pray, speak and walk according to the power of God. I urge you to join me in seeking that power so that you too will hear those breathtaking words,

Well done!
Enter into the joy of your Master!

ENDNOTES

[1] Psalms 91:1 He who dwells in the shelter of the Most High will abide in the shadow of the Almighty.

Chapter 3

What Is This Power?

Thus far, we have identified a problem in the church today. God's power is the force behind everything that happens in His Kingdom, yet that power seems foreign to the body of Christ. The church should be focused on, and accomplishing, the work of the Kingdom, but without God's power, the church cannot fulfill her purpose. She should be the light leading all of society to the cross, yet has become ineffective at influencing society, and is herself being conformed to the world's thinking. When Christians take God's power and use it to live a Kingdom purpose life, people are changed, families thrive, communities strengthen, and the world sees the truth and majesty of Jesus Christ.

I know you desire to be a part of what God is doing in our times. God is giving you a picture of what your family will look like, how marriage works, and why relationships need changing. You see it and you realize this is a game changer for your life. What God is showing you is glorious, sewing seeds of hope for your future. None of it can be done without His power working according to Kingdom principles. All you need is God's power working in your life.

Sounds great, doesn't it? There remains one small detail. You want that power. You recognize you need that power. But what are we really talking about? I mean, what is this power?

According to dictionary.com, the word power has the following meanings:

- ability to do or act; capability of doing or accomplishing something.

- great or marked ability to do or act; strength; might; force.

- the possession of control or command over others; authority; ascendancy:

- legal ability, capacity, or authority:

- delegated authority; authority granted to a person or persons in a particular office or capacity

When discussing God's power, all of these elements come into play, and we will discuss them later in this book. For now, just understand there is an extra element when dealing with God's power. Since God is outside this three-dimensional world, His power contains elements outside the confines of the natural laws of physics. We will discuss this matter in detail in the next chapter. For now, we only need to understand that since this power is beyond our natural laws and limitations, it can manifest to us in our natural world in a number of ways. The most common forms we refer to as miracles or healings, because these are the ones we can actually see. But more happens under God's power than you realize. Provision manifests. People are set free from all sorts of pestering demons, and minds and hearts are protected from their attacks.

None of this is perceived with the human mind. But it is the power of God manifesting nonetheless.

I define God's power this way:

> "It is a natural manifestation in this world resulting when God intervenes beyond or above the principles of nature."

In other words, God's power results in the laws of our three-dimensional world being over-ridden so that what happens is outside the laws of nature. For instance, according to the laws of nature, a grown man cannot be held up by sea water, yet both Peter and Jesus walked on the sea in the middle of a storm.

The Greek word usually translated power is the word "dunamis" which, according to Strong's Concordance, means physical power, force, might, ability, efficacy, energy, powerful deeds, deeds showing (physical) power, marvelous works. In these definitions we see the extra element of works outside our physical laws of nature, with the inclusion of terms such as energy, powerful deeds, and marvelous works. These terms indicate something extraordinary happening compared to normal levels of power.

Now look at what scriptures have to say about God's power.

*And these signs will accompany those who believe:
in my name they will cast out demons;
they will speak in new tongues;
they will pick up serpents with their hands;
and if they drink any deadly poison, it will not hurt them
...they will lay their hands on the sick, and they will recover.*

Mark 16:17-18

With a quick look at this list of actions that follow believers, we see healings, which are tangible manifestations of God's power that we can see. We also see demons being cast out, which we cannot see but is God's power doing something beyond our natural world. I believe that taking up serpents with their hands does not refer to handling physical snakes but refers to handling demonic beings. Remember, Satan is called the serpent and Ephesians 6 tells us that we do not wrestle with flesh and blood but with principalities and authorities of the air. These would again reference God's power beyond what we can perceive. Drinking deadly poison could apply in both the physical and the spiritual realms. The Bible clearly teaches we are not to test God, so we don't do it on purpose to prove something; however, if you are in a situation where something is ingested accidentally or by force, the protection is there. You will not die if you know how to implement this truth. I personally believe this refers to ingesting philosophies of this world, bad doctrines, or demonic influence.

Nothing in this passage can be accomplished without God's power at work in the believers.

Why did Jesus send out believers with the power to do these things?

> *And they went out and preached everywhere,*
> *while the Lord worked with them*
> *and confirmed the message by accompanying signs.*
>
> Mark 16:20

God uses His power through believers' lives to confirm that He is behind everything they represent about His Kingdom. When I teach live seminars, I often tell the audience that if God does not confirm my word with His power, they do not have to receive what I have to say. When He confirms it, all doubt is kicked out the door of their lives and the Word is firmly implanted in their hearts. When I lay hands on the sick and they recover, hearts are opened to the truth of the Word and faith is released in otherwise doubting or misinformed Christians.

Jesus Himself gave the power to His disciples for such signs.

> *And when he had called unto him his twelve disciples,*
> *he gave them power against unclean spirits, to cast them out,*
> *and to heal all manner of sickness*
> *and all manner of disease.*
>
> Matthew 10:1 (KJV)

Jesus tells you as a Christian you are to walk in God's power, and He is the one who made it available to you.

Just before Paul begins a dissertation about being armored up for the battle, he begins with these words:

> *Finally, my brethren, be strong in the Lord,*
> *and in the power of his might.*

> Ephesians 6:10 (KJV)

Paul is keenly aware that there will be no battle won without God's power. Later in verse 12, he tells us that our battle is with specific powers. These powers have an advantage over humans, mainly that humans can neither see nor perceive them. This gives them a clear advantage over humans, but they do not have nearly the ability or power of God. For you to live life being attacked by these powers, you must be strong in the Lord and the power of His might.

Paul said this about his own preaching:

> *and my speech and my message*
> *were not in plausible words of wisdom,*
> *but in demonstration of the Spirit*
> *and of power,*
> *so that your faith might not rest in the wisdom of men*
> *but in the power of God.*

> *1 Corinthians 2:4-5*

Paul fully expected God to confirm his word with power. He was not interested in winning them through logic or argument. He did not intend to sway them with the power of persuasion. All of that is merely human efforts that would lead men to rest in men's work. He spoke the truth of God and let God confirm what he said through demonstrations of the Spirit and of power, so people would put their faith solely on God.

Later in the same letter, Paul referred to some other teachers who were preaching in Corinth.

> *But I will come to you soon, if the Lord wills,*
> *and I will find out*
> *not the talk of these arrogant people*
> *but their power.*
>
> *1 Corinthians 4:19*

Paul could care less what these teachers had to say unless God confirmed them. Paul knew that words can persuade the mind, but only Jesus Christ can change the heart. If Jesus was not on the scene to confirm the words being spoken, the words were virtually worthless.

The very next statement Paul made shook me to the core. It is the very verse that woke me up to the urgency of walking in God's power.

> *For the kingdom of God does not consist in talk*
> *but in power.*
>
> *1 Corinthians 4:20*

To "consist" means to be made up of or composed of. God's Kingdom is composed of His own power and everything in the universe is upheld by that power.

> *and he upholds the universe by the word of his power.*
>
> *Hebrews 1:3*

That's a tremendous amount of power!

In Paul's letter to the Ephesians, he prayed for the "eyes" of their understanding to be opened to specific truths. He wanted them to see what Christians had available to them because of the death and resurrection of Jesus Christ. In this list, the last item Paul prayed for them to understand is this:

> ...*what is the immeasurable greatness of his power toward us who believe,*
>
> *Ephesians 1:19*

I don't know exactly how to quantify that amount of power, but to have an immeasurable portion of something so vast is more than I can wrap my mind around. Are you feeling the same way? Then perhaps, to make sure you don't take this provision lightly, that is why Paul continued:

> *according to the working of his great power that he worked in Christ when he raised him from the dead and seated him at his right hand in the heavenly places,*
>
> *Ephesians 1:19-20*

That amount of power God used to raise Jesus from the dead and seat Him in the highest place of authority in all of heaven is the amount of power that has been made available to you – IF you believe it.

Now, to see how God puts that power to work, look with me at a commonly quoted verse.

> *Now to him who is able to do far more abundantly than all that we ask or think...*
>
> *Ephesians 3:20*

Oh yes! Our God is able to do, not just "abundantly," as if that were not enough, He is able to do *far more* abundantly than anything we ask. He does *far more* abundantly than what we think to ask but don't dare because it would be asking too much. The King James Version says it is "exceedingly" abundant. That is a lot of power our God has, to be able to do so much. No wonder this verse is so popular!

Most people stop right there, but the verse is not finished. The cropped portion carries all the weight of the passage. Take a look:

...according to the power at work within us

Ephesians 3:20

You read that correctly. God's immeasurable greatness of power that is exceedingly abundantly more than you can ask or even think to ask only works when *you* take it and do something with it. God uses Christians to do the work of the Kingdom and He relies on you to step forward, believe and walk it out.

What the Power is Not - A Critical Disclaimer

What I am not

When I talk about utilizing God's power for laying hands on the sick to recover, I am not claiming to have power or the ability to heal sick people. There is only one who heals, who cast out demons and who sets the captives free. His name is Jesus Christ. Jesus is the one who overcame the enemy making a triumph over them. He is the one with the heavenly authority that demons must obey. He is the King that holds the dominion over principalities of the air. I only obey Jesus and do as he tells me, and He works His power through me. I am nothing more than a yielded vessel willing to let Jesus use me like a tool in a tool box for His kingdom work.

What I am

I am a willing vessel, not afraid to pick up that power and do what my King bids me to do. Like David facing Goliath, I know that with the God of Israel's power, I can fearlessly face any giant in my life and slay that enemy.

The Time Has Come

Now is the time to begin revealing secrets you likely did not learn at church, secrets that will enable you to walk in God's power. There has always been a small remnant of believing Christians who walked in the power, yet in the past century, God began raising up an army of believers who dare to take up His power and walk out His Word. The army ranks currently swell with the membership of Saints who take up this mantle, believe God at His Word, and live out their Kingdom purpose life. It is your turn to enlist. You already believe on Jesus Christ for your salvation. Now it is time for you to say, "Lord, here I am! I repent of living by what the world says. From now on, I only live by what you say!"

By expressing those words, you step into an army of Saints on the battlefield. As a member of the army, your Captain of the Hosts wants to reveal battle strategies that lay dormant in most church buildings. These strategies, laid out before the foundation of the world, will provide you with the rest and security available only in Jesus Christ. You will finally enjoy the promises in the Bible as they become real in your life.

One last word of advice before you turn the page. Do not rush through these secrets. Let God have an opportunity to penetrate your mind and your spirit with His everlasting truths. Soak in the scriptures provided. Give yourself an opportunity to get a "lightbulb" moment of understanding from the Holy Spirit. Test my words. Take them to the Lord and ask Him for yourself. Go to the Bible and search for yourself.

Everything I present to you in this book, God has confirmed with demonstrations of His power at various live events and speaking engagements. That is confirmation for me, to be assured of what I bring to the people in His name. I encourage you to test everything in the Spirit of God, so that when God brings you the understanding, then your faith will rest in Him, and not in my words.

Chapter 4

Secret Number One

The Power Source

You have come a long way in your understanding of God's power and why it is critical for Christians to utilize it. It is only through God's power the church can function in the way she is called. This power equips the church to produce results exceedingly abundantly more than we ask or think. All we need do is listen to God and do what He leads us to do. As we obey, He provides His power and does the job Himself. We are yielded vessels, allowing God to use us like a tool to accomplish his Kingdom work. This power manifests through the Holy Spirit, Who does works beyond our natural laws, such as when He raised Jesus from the dead.

Now that we understand the power, we need to be clear about the source of the power. We know, generally speaking, the source of the power is God Himself; however, we need to understand a little more about the nature of His kingdom, because we learned in the previous chapter that his kingdom consists of His power (or is made up of or composed of His power). We must look closer at this kingdom, so we may understand the source of the power.

Secret Number One

You must understand the Kingdom of God because it is the source of the power

Time for a Shift

Are you familiar with the term paradigm? It is the way in which you perceive a matter. Steve Covey popularized the term paradigm shift in his famous book, *The 7 Habits of Highly Effective People* published in 1989, where he described a study on paradigm shifts published by Harvard University. A paradigm shift is when you realize that what you have been perceiving can be looked at a totally different way. Let me show you an example from the Bible.

In 2 Kings chapter 6, there is a story of Elisha the prophet. God has been revealing the war plans of the Syrian army to Elisha who would take that information to his king so the Israelites could counter the planned Syrian attacks. Once the Syrian king realizes his plans are continuously exposed, and identifies Elisha as the source, he amasses a great army to go into the city and seize the prophet.

Elisha's personal servant, upon seeing the great army surrounding the city, knows they are amassing to take his master, Elisha. To calm his terrified servant, Elisha makes a strange statement.

> *"Do not be afraid,*
> *for those who are with us*
> *are more than those who are with them."*
>
> 2 Kings 6:16

What an unusual response to the situation! These two men alone face a great army, yet Elisha says, "Those who are with us are more." The servant only sees two men - himself and his master - facing myriads of soldiers before them.

> *Then Elisha prayed and said,*
> *"O LORD, please open his eyes that he may see."*
>
> 2 Kings 6:17

I think it is obvious the servant's eyes are wide open already. He is horrified by the sight before him! Apparently, Elisha had another kind of "seeing" in mind. There was something Elisha knew, something his servant was unaware of, something that was beyond what the servant was already perceiving. In other words, Elisha was perceiving something the servant was not. Elisha had a different paradigm – a different way of "seeing" the situation.

The Harvard Study used a picture of a lady. In this picture, the lady could look young or old, depending on how you perceived it, and how you perceived it depended on how you were preconditioned by being exposed to previous pictures, whether of a young lady or of an old lady.

Elisha's servant was preconditioned to see the natural world. It is all he had been exposed to and all he knew. Elisha had been conditioned by knowing and believing his God. This gave Elisha a different view of the situation.

> *So the LORD opened the eyes of the young man,
> and he saw, and behold,
> the mountain was full of horses and chariots of fire
> all around Elisha.*
>
> 2 Kings 6:17

Christians are preconditioned by the natural world because that is all we have been exposed to. The Kingdom of God exists outside those natural limitations, and we need a paradigm shift in order to "see" it. This requires being "exposed" to the truth of God's Word long enough so that you believe it to the point that you believe it even when the natural world seems to conflict with it.

In the case of Elisha and his servant, the truth of God's promised protection and provision (a heavenly host with chariots of fire) conflicted with the natural truth (two men standing alone). A choice had to be made. Which will you perceive? Which will you believe? The servant perceived only the natural. Elisha perceived both the natural and the supernatural (above or beyond the natural) then he made a choice to walk according to the supernatural, the one that existed based on the truth of God's Word.

It is important to note that both paradigms were true. The natural was true because two men stood alone facing the Syrian army. The supernatural was also true because God assigned an entire host to protect Elisha. These were not opposing paradigms but overlapping ones. Both were true at the same time. This is a critical point to understand.

We live in both paradigms. Both are true, but we must choose which one we will live by. As was the case with Elisha, they will most often conflict. When they do, you must choose.

To conclude the story from 2 Kings, Elisha and his servant conquered the Syrian army. When the army came down to take Elisha, Elisha prayed for them to be blinded, and once they were, he led the entire lot to his king, then prayed their sight to be restored. When the King asked if he should slay them all, Elisha told the king to feed them instead and send them home. It would not have happened that way if Elisha had not had a different paradigm than what he saw in the natural. Had he walked by the natural, he would have been dead before the sun went down. Instead, the whole nation of Israel was set free from a dangerous neighbor because, from that day forward, the Syrians never messed with them again. All of this was the result of one man seeing the situation from another perspective – God's paradigm.

Once you begin to see life with a new supernatural paradigm, you will have taken a major step in preparing yourself to be a very powerful Christian. This new paradigm has a familiar name. It is called the Kingdom of God. The Bible tells us to seek first the Kingdom of God and everything you need will be added unto you. This was certainly the case in Elisha's story.

Sounds easy, but a major problem pops up right here. You will not find the Kingdom of God in the natural world. It is here, but you cannot see it with your natural eyes or perceive it with your intellect. How will you find this Kingdom that you seek? How will you know if you found it?

It will take a paradigm shift.

I will now begin to shift your paradigm so you can "see" the Kingdom of God.

It's a Numbers Game

Our world consists of three dimensions:

1) Depth
2) Width
3) Height

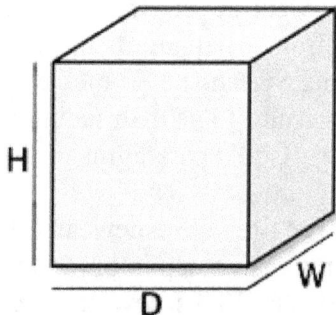

Depth, width and height are referred to as dimensions. If you take a box down to the post office to mail it, they will want to know its dimensions. You will give them the measurements of the depth, the width and the height of the box. With that information, they will calculate the volume of the box. This is what is meant by dimensions, and these three dimensions encompass our entire natural world.

In the fascinating science of quantum physics, scientists claim to have proved nine dimensions. I salute all the quantum physicists out there because they understand things I will never get my brain around. I cannot begin to get a grip on any dimensions beyond the three that exist in the physical realm as described above.

But proved they are, nonetheless, with a claim of potentially eleven dimensions currently the popular consensus. Knowing my God, there could be hundreds of dimensions. I would not be the least surprised if it is so.

Assuming there are nine total dimensions, and knowing I can only perceive three dimensions, I quickly ascertain that, at best, I can only perceive one third of all reality. Two thirds of all reality are somewhere outside those three dimensions that make up our natural world.

Humans utilize five senses to perceive these three dimensions.

1) Sight
2) Hearing
3) Touch
4) Smell
5) Taste

With these five senses, we perform our task of perceiving our natural physical three-dimensional world.

Have you heard someone say, "I'll believe it when I see it!" Perhaps they have not considered that there is more to life than what we can perceive with our five senses.

I have a dog whistle and my Labrador retriever can take commands from that whistle a quarter of a mile away. If you were standing 10 feet away, you would not hear even the hissing sound (the only part of the whistle that humans can hear). This begs the question: If you cannot hear the whistle, does that mean there is not really any sound extending from it? You might not hear it, but the proof that the sound does extend that far away is when my dog proves she hears it when she obeys its command.

You have all matter of unperceived realities bombarding you daily. They are real, whether you perceive them or not. Radio and television waves surround you right now. You cannot perceive them, but they are there. You cannot hear them, see them, taste them, touch them or smell them. Does this mean they are not real? You need only turn on a device that detects and translates them to prove they are there. Tune your radio or your television and you will hear or see how real they are. They are real. You just cannot perceive them in our three-dimensional world using your five senses.

In those many dimensions that you cannot perceive, there are all manner of beings you cannot see, hear, taste, touch or smell. Angels exist that have been assigned to minister to you and war over you. Just because you cannot see them, does not mean they are not real. The enemy lurks hidden behind that veil, seeking whom he may devour. Just because you cannot see Satan or demons does not mean they are not real. In our story from 2 Kings 6, Elisha's servant had a brief glimpse at just how real these beings are.

This is why the Word of God is so very important. It reminds me of the old minefields of modern wars. Do you remember how they worked? An army takes an explosive device called a mine and plants it just under the surface of the ground in an area they expect their enemy to pass through. It is designed to detonate if weight is placed upon it. Often, a field or open area would be littered with mines. If you walk through that field, you would have no idea of the unseen dangers lurking under the sand, just beyond your perception – until someone in your platoon steps on one. Then everyone is aware! The only problem? You can't even turn and run back from where you came. You don't know where they are hidden. You may have just stepped over one only a few paces back. What a terrifying situation!

What if, at that very moment, you had a walkie talkie. On the other end of that walkie talkie is another person who knows where every mine is buried. On that day, your walkie talkie would be your most prized procession. You would never set that radio down. You would be sure the batteries were charged. You would have the squelch set just right so that you would not miss a single word spoken by the person who could lead you out of your treacherous situation.

I believe this is a picture of your life. You are walking through landmines of dangers lurking outside of your ability to perceive them. Stepping on one could prove dangerous, even fatal. But you have been given a walkie talkie, an ability to communicate, with One Who knows where every landmine is buried. He knows every trick and trap laid out against you.

There should never be a time when you ignore your walkie talkie. You must keep it in your hands always - talking, listening, following every word precisely – because it is your only hope of avoiding terrible dangers.

I believe this is what Paul meant when he said,

"...pray without ceasing..."

1 Thessalonians 5:17

When you think the natural world is all there is to reality, the Bible is not really so important. We would say it is important, since it is God's Word and we should all live by it, but most Christians do not give it a critical level of priority in their life. Once you realize

- there is more than the natural world,
- that most of reality is beyond our ability to perceive it,

- myriads of dangers have a target on you,
- and there is only One Who can help you avoid those dangers,

there is a paradigm shift. God's Word becomes the *only* hope of getting through the minefield we call "life." It becomes the only source of life, hope, protection, provision and rescue. You will keep your radio (your heart) sharply tuned to His frequency so that you do not miss even one word of what He speaks. His will becomes your will. His desires become your desires. Nothing the world has to offer is worth giving up the hope you have in God and His Word.

*And the Word became flesh
and dwelt among us*

John 1:14

God's spoken Word was manifested into a physical three-dimensional body and dwelt among us in this natural world. The frequency you need to keep your radio tuned to is called Jesus Christ. He is your only hope of navigating this life.

Think about the minefield as you read this popular passage of scripture.

*"The thief comes only to steal and kill and destroy.
I came that they may have life
and have it abundantly."*

John 10:10

Is this shifting your paradigm a bit?

How to Walk on Water

To shift your paradigm a little more, I want you to consider the story of Jesus walking on the water. It is one of the more popular stories in the Bible and found in nearly every children's Bible story books. But few consider that Jesus was not the only one who walked on water that night.

The story takes place in the night after a long day of teaching and ministering to a large crowd. Jesus sent his disciples ahead in a boat to cross to the other side. During the night, the wind was against the boat. As the disciples feared their dire situation, a figure was seen walking across the water right out there in the middle of the sea! Once they realized it was Jesus, bold Peter said,

> *"Lord, if it is you, command me to come to you on the water."*
>
> *Matthew 14:28*

Jesus answered by commanding him, "Come." Peter then got out of the boat and walked on the water going straight to Jesus!

Something happened along the way. Peter began to notice the wind. As a sailor, I know how challenging it can be when offshore in a storm. Wind kicks up seas, and seas swamp boats. Night brings an eeriness, as you cannot see the waves coming your way. As wave after unseen wave takes you by surprise, fear begins to creep in. You feel like you are at the mercy of the sea. Peter is in a boat in this type of situation where the entire crew is concerned for the safety of the vessel. What does Peter do? He gets out of the boat!

Peter quickly begins to reconsider his decision. The reality of the waves and the danger they bring suddenly strikes him. As fear sets in, he begins to sink.

Peter is in trouble, big trouble. I am certain that the waves were pounding down on him and making it hard to breath and stay afloat. He looks to Jesus and cries, "Lord, save me!" I can imagine how intently he had his eyes fixed on Jesus. Just like a man drowning in a pool looking desperately to the lifeguard for rescue, Peter was certainly looking desperately at Jesus, his only hope of survival.

Jesus comes to him and lifts him back on top of the water, where Peter is able to walk back to the boat and climb inside.

Walking on water is a supernatural event that is outside the physical laws of nature. As long as Peter had his eyes fixed on Jesus he was able to walk on the water. As soon as his attention was off Jesus and on his circumstances, he began to sink. When his eyes were back on Jesus, he was back on top of that water.

Where are your eyes? If they are on Jesus, you will be able to operate outside the natural elements of this three-dimensional world. You will be operating in the Kingdom of God, the source of God's power, able to walk on top of circumstances in your life. If you step on landmines, they will not detonate, or you will incur little to no damage from them.

Take your eyes off Jesus and the supernatural is no longer available to you. In the natural world, you are drowning in your circumstances and don't understand why. You pray and nothing happens. It is because your radio is not tuned to the correct frequency. You do not have your eyes fixed on the Word of God, Jesus Christ, your only hope. You are not operating in the Kingdom of God where the power source is, the power that is beyond this three-dimensional world and is not confined by the physical laws of nature – a power that can set you on top of your circumstances.

Here is a quick summary:

> <u>Eyes fixed on Jesus</u> – You are walking in supernatural power, operating in God's Kingdom.
>
> <u>Eyes off Jesus</u> – you are walking in the natural, drowning in your circumstances, with no power available.

Now apply that to dealing with your enemy,

> *For we do not wrestle against flesh and blood,*
> *but against the rulers,*
> *against the authorities,*
> *against the cosmic powers over this present darkness,*
> *against the spiritual forces of evil in the heavenly places.*
>
> *Ephesians 6:12*

This passage describes an enemy hidden just beyond your ability to perceive them. This scripture reveals mines in the field you cannot see. This enemy seeks to kill, steal and destroy your life, your family, your marriage, your children, your work. How will you battle such an enemy, one that you cannot perceive?

If you deal with this enemy by using your five senses according to the natural world, you are already sunk. You are defeated. This is because the natural is where Satan has his temporary reign. You battle on his turf, giving him home field advantage.

If you deal with this enemy by the Word of God, you battle an enemy that is already defeated in Jesus Christ.

> *He disarmed the rulers and authorities*
> *and put them to open shame,*
> *by triumphing over them in him.*
>
> *Colossians 2:15*

Battling this enemy in the Kingdom of God is battling fully armored with God's power at your disposal. It is your choice. You will not "happen" into supernatural power. You must choose it, and you choose it by determining to live by God's paradigm, just as Elisha did. Your choice will affect every area of your life because the enemy wants to destroy every part of your life.

God has exposed the landmines. He has His radio waves transmitting to you. It is up to you to tune your heart to His Word, because it is the only gateway you have to access the power source, the Kingdom of God.

You now have the first powerful secret revealed. By now, you should be starting to "see" the Kingdom of God, which is the very source of God's power. Because you have begun a paradigm shift, you are ready to look at the second secret that is rarely taught in churches. In many ways, it builds upon what you have just learned. Once you take the next secret and combine it with this first secret, you will be ready to start the "how to" secrets that will open the door to God's power coming forth in your life.

Chapter 5

Secret Number Two

Keep Your Keys in Your Pocket

You now have your new paradigm and are ready to learn how to be powerful in God's Kingdom. Before you went through the last chapter, you would not have had the ability to understand what I share in this chapter. You needed that paradigm shift as a precursor for anything going forward to make sense. You must grasp the existence of supernatural dimensions – those dimensions that exist beyond the three that you are able to perceive.

You may consider pausing here in this book and going back to reread chapter four. Reread it as many times as needed so your paradigm shifts completely and your spiritual eyes open to the reality of those other dimensions, because it is in those supernatural dimensions where God's Kingdom exists and all His work takes place. Take your time. This is a life changing moment and you want to allow God as much time as He wants, so this truth solidifies in you.

Are you ready to continue?

Secret Number Two

To unlock the power, you need three keys that ensure your faith is in the right place

The next secret encompasses three important concepts I want you to remember. Tuck them away in your heart. Write them on index cards and carry them with you if you need to. Revisit this chapter periodically so they don't slip away from you. These are the golden keys to unlocking God's power in your life, and you do not want to lose your keys!

Key Number One
Human Power Fails

Human power always fails. It may look good to other people. It may seem to accomplish great things at times. But it has no effect in the Kingdom of God.

> ...and all our righteous acts are like filthy rags;
>
> Isaiah 64:6 (NIV)

This may be one of the most mis-quoted scriptures of the whole Bible. I mostly hear it spoken something like this, "And all our sin is like filthy rags." Notice there is a remarkable difference between what most people *think* this verse says and what it actually says. God is not commenting on our sin at all. He is commenting on the best deeds man can possibly produce. Why would God say the best deeds you do are as valueless as filthy rags?

Deeds may appear remarkable to other humans, but any actions or deeds done outside of God's will are done outside of His Kingdom. Human actions are based on the tiny amount of reality we perceive in our limited three dimensions. God's deeds are based on all reality. God sees in all the dimensions; therefore, God is the only one who can determine proper courses of action to successfully achieve His will.

In addition, the human heart is fallible. From the time of the fall of man in the garden, the thinking of man has been skewed. Therefore, scriptures teach us we must be renewed in our minds into the likeness of Jesus Christ[1] so that we can once again think like Jesus thinks. Humans can be fooled by our own hearts, because we can be deceived in our hearts.

Look at what Jesus said concerning the heart:

"You are those who justify yourselves before men,
but God knows your hearts.
For what is exalted among men
is an abomination in the sight of God."

Luke 16:15

Humans accomplish marvelous things for God at times. To other humans, these acts can have the appearance of power, as they seem to be accomplishing mighty things that look like God's work. Impressive deeds cause people to exalt each other. Be careful! When you receive praises from others, you tend to take that as a cue you are doing well. Your goal is not impressing other humans, but in doing the will of your Father in heaven, the only One whose deeds are pure righteous deeds, truly valuable deeds that accomplish real solid lasting results.

Behind that veil, in the dimensions where most of reality takes place, God's will and deeds are all that matter. God accomplishes the working of His will by utilizing His power in the lives of yielded humans. These humans do amazingly marvelous deeds, but they are God's deeds, performed by God's power according to God's will.

The true test of the work is not in how great it looks to man, but if it was done according to God's will. If God was not in that work, that work will fail. Huge successful looking ministries have failed because the heart of the minister was not grounded in seeking God's will but was self-serving. Any self-serving work has no effect in the Kingdom of God and actually proves to be counterproductive in the long term.

This is just as true for the little things you and I do every day. I have learned that anything I do outside God's will and destiny for my life is doomed for failure. I do not want to waste one minute doing anything destined for doom. I want every effort to be successful and powerful for the Kingdom. When I guard my deeds, making sure everything I do accords with God's will, I enjoy God's promised results in my marriage, my parenting, and my ministry.

Your human effort will fail. You must be sure that everything you do is according to God's will. It must be God's work, God's way and God's power. When you learn to do everything God's way, Bible promises are assured in every area of your life. Learn to let God have His way. As soon as you learn to let loose of your will, desires and passions, you gain the ability to access God's power and all your efforts will be successful, because God's works never fail.

Key Number Two
Know Who's Doing What

If your own works are fruitless filthy rags in the Kingdom of God but God's works are pure and powerful, then you had better be sure whose work you are really doing.

I conduct weekend retreats where I teach people how to become powerful Christians. One of the many things learned is the right of Christians to lay hands on the sick for healing. In the very first session I make this statement, "I cannot teach you how to heal the sick because I have never healed anyone in my life!" This is a true statement. Many times, I have laid my hands on the sick and they recover, but I did not heal them. There is only one healer, and his name is Jesus Christ. One of the Hebrew names for God is YHWH (Yahweh) Rapha, The Lord is my healer. He alone heals, and I am certain I have no ability to do such deeds myself.

Any miracle God does through my hand, I know it is Him, His power, and His authority. For you to be a powerful Christian, you must yield to Him and walk according to His kingdom principles. You must see yourself, not as the miracle worker, but as a tool in the hands of the true miracle worker. The real work is going on behind the veil in those other dimensions, and you are only doing His bidding for the small part that must transpire on this side of the veil.

Key Number Three
Put Your Faith in the Right Place

When deeds are accomplished, most of the work is out of sight to humans, behind the veil in the supernatural realm. If you cannot see in the place where most of the work is done, how foolish it would be to think you could figure out what to do by sizing up the situation and making your own decisions about how to handle it. Only God sees on both sides of the veil, so only He can call the shots and determine how to handle situations. This is what the Bible means when it says:

The righteous shall live by faith.

Romans 1:17

****

And the life I now live in the flesh I live by faith

Galatians 2:20

****

But my righteous one shall live by faith

Hebrews 10:38

No matter what situation you encounter in life, you respond to it according to the Word of God, because God knows the only solution that works. When you do this, His power is there boosting your deed, making sure of its success. You do not live according to what your eyes tell you, you live by faith in the Word of God and what He tells you, because His eyes see so much more than yours do.

Remember Elisha's choice in 2 Kings chapter 6? He had to choose between the limited three-dimensional natural world that his eyes could see, and the supernatural dimensions where God had already spoken. He was choosing between what he could see (living by sight) and faith in God (God would never leave him or forsake him). When he chose to live by faith, it released all the power of heaven to work on his behalf and the outcome was obviously well beyond anything the natural world could have produced for him.

You will find many times you face decisions like Elisha's. It may not appear so life threatening, but you will face circumstances where you could have a natural response (such as yelling at a nasty person) or a God response (using a soft answer to turn away wrath).[2] Just like Elisha, you must choose if you will live by this natural limited world, or if you will live by faith in what God says, believing every word that proceeds out of His mouth.

Your human power is weak, unreliable, and fails you at every turn. Only God's supernatural power is strong, perfect, and accomplishes its goal every time. You must decide whether you will rely on your own petty thoughts and deeds, or on the perfect knowledge of Most High God who sees all and knows all in every dimension of reality. Trust Him at His Word above any situation or circumstance you encounter in this world.

You now have a new set of keys in your possession. Keep these three keys in your pocket. Never lose them. They unlock the door to power flowing in your life and your family.

These three keys have prepared your heart to receive the power of God. The next secret I reveal will discipline your mind to function in that power.

ENDNOTES

[1]Colossians 3:10 and have put on the new self, which is being renewed in knowledge after the image of its creator.

[2]Proverbs 15:1 A soft answer turns away wrath, but a harsh word stirs up anger.

Chapter 6

Secret Number Three

A Common Thread

You may have spent much of your Christian life wondering why your prayers never get answered, why you don't see God's promises in your life, and why your life isn't more powerful. You read about the New Testament church and long for your Christian life to have that kind of power. You admire other Christians who do great things for the Lord. You want to grow into the maturity it takes to be like that. But you realize it takes time, lots of time, to get to that point.

This is true. It does take time. But this does not mean sitting around living life as usual while you wait for those weekly trips to church to finally take effect. People who are waiting for maturity in Christ like that will only see minimal changes in their life, even after decades of diligently keeping the Sunday schedule. I know people who have shown up for church, sung unto the Lord, agreed with the Pastor, and participated in prayer with earnest. But 30 years of this fervor from the pew yielded only little growth.

Yes, it will take time, but the trick is how you spend your time. Those who grow to power in God generally have several things in common about their use of time.

Secret Number Three

There are common elements in the lives of Christians who experience God's power

I was in that place. I wanted maturity, but I sensed pew sitting, though important, was only a small part of a bigger picture. I began studying the powerful people, the ones I know and the public figures that had a long-term running record. How did they get so mature? What did they have in common?

I discovered areas that overlapped in the lives of these people. As I began to implement some of these characteristics in my life, the changes began. At first, I wondered if there would be any effect as I could detect little to no change. Many times, I caught myself falling back into old routines and needed to start over. Mostly I needed perseverance with my mind set on moving forward no matter what.

The results of a little tenacity set my life on fire. I now enjoy the promises of God's Word with all its peace, joy and abundant life. I have an uncontainable zeal for the things of God and my prayer life shakes the heavens.

I want to share with you this common thread I found and implemented, the one that lit the path I currently tread in this new Kingdom life.

*Every powerful Christian understands
there is no life and no purpose
outside the Kingdom of God
and how they prioritize their time reflects this.*

Powerful Christians do not just make time for the things of God. They live every part of their life by the Word of God. One man once commented to me, "I don't choose which socks to wear until I talk with God about it." Sounds extreme, and perhaps it is. Yet once you realize the Kingdom is outside our three-dimensional world and every source of help - and every danger - abides there, out of your vision or perception, you will take every matter in your life to God and won't decide or act without Him. Remember the minefield. God is the only One Who can lead you through a life full of unseen dangers and through doors of opportunity. He alone keeps you safe, puts you in the right place for success, provides in any situation, and empowers you for everything you must accomplish. He is the only hope for your marriage, your children, and every circumstance no matter how foreboding or impossible it seems to you.

Often when I speak at seminars, I introduce myself by holding up my Bible and pronouncing, "This is who I live for. I am a disciple of Jesus Christ. I eat this Word, sleep this Word, live this Word. It is my life, my breath, my very substance. Without it, I have no life, no hope, and no direction."

That is how I view my life. I do not live by sight (the natural circumstances of life) but I live by faith (believing God's Word no matter what my logical mind tells me about my situation). I know that most of what takes place in life happens behind the veil. I do not expect to see how situations unfold so I do not make decisions on what I see in the natural. I simply trust God and respond how He wants me to, and then I rest in Him, knowing that His ways always work. The outcome of any situation is His problem, not mine, *if* I do things according to Kingdom principles.

With this perception of life, the Kingdom of God becomes the highest priority. You don't just "make time" for God, you crave it. You know you cannot make a move without it. Jesus becomes a part of every decision and every reaction to every situation.

When the Kingdom of God becomes the highest priority, things of God become a daily part of life, not a block of time on your weekly calendar. No longer is God a Sunday thing with a little sprinkle of Wednesday night. He is a minute by minute thing. Powerful Christians live a daily life with Jesus. Here are just a few of the ways this could play out in your home.

More Than Church on Sunday

Our family has church most every day in our home, as do many powerful Christians. We sing songs of worship, have time of learning from the scriptures, and prayer time together out loud where every member of the family participates. In these teaching times, our children are not simply fed cute Bible stories or quick devotions. They learn how to live their life prioritizing the Kingdom of God. They learn what it means to trust God instead of trusting their emotions. They learn all the accomplishments of the death and resurrection of Jesus Christ. They learn how to apply God's Word to their own decision making, and how their decisions and actions affect other people. Because they have been so ingrained in God's Word, the power flows mightily through them. Quite often, at church or on other corporate gatherings, my children are called upon to pray for others before I am.[1]

In addition to this corporate gathering in our home, each child is encouraged to have their own private and intimate time with God. I set an example for the children by letting them see my daily time with God. They know the particular chair I use in my bedroom for God time, and I leave the bedroom door open so they see me sitting there, reading, praying, singing, or down on my knees. Sometimes I spend that time in our living room, to give them more opportunity to see, or to perhaps join in.

In addition to this daily time focused on Jesus Christ, we have a weekly time to gather for worship. Every Friday night we put on worship music, sing, dance and praise God together. Many powerful Christian families have such worship times so their members stay focused on the majesty and mercy of our mighty God. This is not a time to ask God for anything, but to lift Him up in the eyes of our children and just worship Him for who He is.

During these weekly worship sessions, we take communion as a family, led by my husband. If he is not available due to his travel schedule, I lead the children. Some think a pastor must administer communion, but this is man's tradition. The Bible says to do it often to remember the body and blood of Jesus Christ. You do not need a pastor for that. I know people who take communion every day. Smith Wigglesworth, one of the most powerful Christians of modern history, took communion every day because he said it was the greatest exchange ever made. He wanted to be sure to think upon it every day without fail.

There are many other ways households live out a daily life in God's Kingdom. I know families who choose a corporate day of fasting. For instance, every Thursday until sundown, the household members refrain from eating, to train their bodies that God is their master, not their stomachs. Some families set aside one hour a day for Bible reading. Sometimes this hour is spent taking turns reading out loud. Other times each family member goes to a quiet place to read on their own. Either way, the Bible has priority for that hour daily.

Won't work in My House!

When sharing these ideas with families at seminars and churches, I have some parents respond with giggles, if not total disdain, at the thought of starting such practices in their homes. They tell me how their children will scoff, laugh, or think the whole thing stupid. I encourage them that their children's perception is not such an important factor. After all, they only see it from a natural viewpoint. Once you understand the dangers for your children outside the shelter of Most High God, you will not make your household decisions based on their opinions, you will make them based on God and His promised protection.

This is usually only an issue with teenagers. Younger children expect to do what the parents do and naturally follow along. Pre-teens and teenagers may think it strange at first, but after you speak with them about why you are doing this, and when they see your consistency and determination, the awkwardness will begin to fade, and eventually they will be a more willing participant. You might start without requiring them to join in. After a while invite them to voluntarily join you. Let them see you do it so they can get accustomed to it. Give them a timeframe when they can expect you will require them to join you. Then stick to it. They may resist, complain, or not know what to do, but with your example and the love of Jesus in you, (and your prayers) they should settle into it. No matter their reaction, you do what you know is right before the Lord, and let God deal with your children's reactions. If you have a teenager who obstinately refuses, just keep yourself on the path. No lecture is as effective as witnessing your example of daily perseverance. More than anything, you must demonstrate an attitude of joy. Fussing and squawking will not draw them in. Your peace and the Holy Spirit will.

Just For Yourself

You cannot model for your family what you do not have for yourself. The only way to experience the power of God in your life is to abide in Jesus Christ. Jesus Himself would leave the crowd and go up into the mountain to pray. He separated Himself from the needs of the people and the work of the Kingdom to refresh in the presence of the Father. If Jesus needed to do this, how much more do we as humans need to spend time in the presence of God.

I regularly set time apart just for getting in the presence of God. Often, I put on worship music and grab my Bible and just let the Holy Spirit lead me. When I first began, it all felt awkward, and I was uncertain what I should do. I developed a routine to get me started, and over time, I learned how to let the Holy Spirit lead me.

When I was starting out, I did not have the convenience of current technology such as mobile devices. I used cd's in a cd player and had to stop to switch songs. Today, I create playlists that run straight through. I then use my device to pause the song or change the volume according to the leading of the Spirit, which can be very convenient when you are down on the floor.

I like to start with upbeat praise songs, almost like a celebration of God. As the music set continues, I choose quieter, more worshipful songs and quite often end up humbling myself before Him either on my knees or flat on my belly.

During these times, I ask nothing of God. I only praise Him for Who He is. The Holy Spirit reminds me of scriptures that reveal things about Him and I worship Him for things as the Spirit leads. If the Spirit places a particular person on my heart, I will pray for them and ask God for their needs to be met, but I refrain from asking for anything for myself.

I stay in the presence of God until I feel He releases me. These sessions usually last from one to three hours but have occasionally lasted even longer. Sure, I get disruptions sometimes. I have a family, so it comes with the territory. I do not fret or get aggravated, I am simply thankful for the time I did get, even if it was only a few minutes.

Times spent like this with the Lord have proven to be some of my sweetest memories of intimacy with the Father. With time and diligence, God has given me much revelation, has interpreted scriptures to me and has revealed His heart toward other people or situations. He has used visions to reveal how fathomless His love is for me and for others. He has shown me how to love the loveless, help the helpless, and overcome my numerous human failings.

Every powerful Christian has some way they spend large amounts of time in the presence of God. It is the only way to know His heart, His will, and the direction He needs you to go. He prepares your heart and mind to handle the power once it begins to flow. Some have special places in their home or on their property they set aside as a meeting place for them and

God. Some want music. Others want the sounds of nature, or a quiet place that allows God to place His own song in their heart. Some travel to quiet destinations to spend days or weeks in the presence.

It doesn't matter how you spend the time with God, or where you decide to spend it. The important thing is to do it. You may wonder how to find such time in your busy schedule. If you are serious about maturing in Jesus Christ and living a powerful Christian life, then it must become a priority. When I first started, I put my young children to bed and went to bed with my husband. Soon as my husband was asleep, I would get up, go into the living room and pray, worship, or read my Bible according to the routine I shared with you previously. It cost me some sleep, but I decided I would rather be tired with God's presence than to be more rested without it. I left it up to God to redeem my rest time or show me another time to meet with Him.

One time, my husband woke up and went looking for me. When he found me on the living room floor, he joined me, and from that time on, we spent time in the Lord together at an earlier time.

I have shared with you a common thread woven throughout the lives of Christians who experience the power of God in their lives. It is between you and God to decide how this will look in your life and your family. Do not brush this off or take it lightly. Time with God is time tapping into the source of your very life. In a Kingdom, time with the King is a tremendous honor. Do not miss your opportunity to walk in that place. The changes in your life over time will astound you.

Think of It This Way

I know life is busy, but you can save yourself a lot of extra work and stress if you will simply block time to spend with Jesus Christ. Assess all the things that beckon for your time. Are they things God assigned you to accomplish? There should be nothing on your full plate that is not His doing. Anything else could be robbing you of the precious time you need to spend with God.

I heard a story once about a man who was chopping down a tree. Another fellow walked by, and after observing the tree chopper, commented, "Looks like you have a dull axe. You should sharpen that blade." The tree chopper replied, "I don't have time. I'm too busy chopping down this tree!"

Is this your life? Are you expending tremendous amounts of energy and time that are being wasted because you won't stop and "sharpen your blade?" Time with God will sharpen you, refocus you on the important priorities in life, and give you a clear understanding of God's heart and His purpose for you.

You are vitally important to the Kingdom of God. Satan will do anything to sidetrack you from God's plan. If he can keep you spinning your wheels on unimportant things, he can easily wreck your time. It is up to you to sharpen your blade and keep your life laser focused on what Jesus Christ prioritizes. Spending time with God is the only way to stay sharp in His Kingdom so you can slice through the work He sets before you.

Time to Get the Power

You should be absorbing most of what I have shown you so far. Do not be concerned if you do not understand it all. It takes time to process so much information. You may need to go back to different chapters to remember what has been said so far. I recommend taking different sections of the book and spending time with God in the scriptures asking Him to help you "see" His Kingdom.

If you feel ready to proceed, it is time to begin the process of building up the power of God in your life. It is accomplished in much the same way you would build power in your body, by building your spiritual muscles.

Building muscles takes time. The same exercises must be repeated over and over until the muscles build. At first you won't see much difference, yet you will notice that you can lift a little more weight than you did at the start. The power begins to grow and eventually you see a difference in how your muscles look when they begin to bulk up. The same holds true with your spiritual muscles. You may not notice the power building at first, but you will eventually see your spiritual strength growing.

In the gym, there are many workout stations, each one designed to work a different muscle group. If you ignore the upper body and only work the lower, you will have strong legs to pick up heavy weight but lack the arm strength to contain it. Only if you work all the stations will you experience total body strength and reap the greatest benefits of your workouts.

These truths hold true for your spiritual muscles as well. The next three secrets will be like workout stations of specific truths of God's Kingdom that you will work out with over and over until you gain the needed strength in that area to contain the power and properly utilize it. Don't give up. To quit is to lose all the muscles you have gained. If you do not give up, you will begin to see the power starting to work in your life.

You cannot choose one of the truths and ignore the rest. It is imperative you work with all of them because they are interrelated. Using any one without the others is like using only a part of your body to lift and contain the weight. God offers you the immeasurable greatness of his power. You must prepare yourself to utilize it or you will compromise it.

As I reveal these next secrets, I recommend you learn them in the order presented. Feel free to read through all of them to get familiar with them, but then go back to begin working with them. Build up your spiritual muscles in one until you feel the strength, then go to the next to begin working with it. This is important because you will need to renew your mind in each of these individual truths. Keep repeating them all so you grow in them together. Just like at the gym, you must work at all the stations repeatedly to reap the most benefit. Start slow and build up as you feel ready. In time, you will be spiritually stronger doing greater and greater things in the Kingdom of God.

Reading this book is the beginning of the process for you. Once you complete it, you will begin seeing Gods power in your life. You will not complete the book, place it on a shelf, and turn on God's power like a switch. You must continue to renew your mind in these truths, building your spiritual muscles more and more. [2]

A relative of mine used to attend Real Estate seminars. Thousands of people would pay hundreds of dollars to attend these seminars, all chasing the hope of making bundles of money. Woven into the words of the teachers at these seminars were truths of how to create wealth or passive income with Real Estate. All the attendees heard all the same truth about how it is done. Most believed what they heard and understood how wealth could be achieved through Real Estate.

Yet, if you surveyed the attendees one year later, you would find that approximately 95% of those attendees had not created one bit of wealth or one dollar of passive income in the 12 months since they attended the seminar and heard those truths. As a matter of fact, many would attend seminar after seminar, yet not create any passive income or add to their wealth.

Does this indicate that the seminars were terrible and just didn't work? Not necessarily. There were 5% who did walk out of a seminar and created wealth for themselves. Were these small handful of people simply smarter than all the rest? It is possible. But I think the difference between the 95% who accomplished nothing but emptying their wallets of hundreds of dollars and the 5% who created wealth and income is simply this – the 5% acted.

Hearing the truth about Real Estate gave every single attendee of the conference knowledge of the truth. Most of them believed what they were taught and understood how it works. Only a handful of them took that knowledge and did something with it. These few exercised their knowledge and it set them on their way to producing larger muscles – in this case, their wealth.

So many Christians sit in church and hear the truth week after week, year after year. Christians spend multiple millions of dollars every year on books, DVDs and conferences all teaching about the Word of God and how to live as a Christian. Never in history has there been so much knowledge of God's Word available to every Christian. But the largest percent of Christians are only hearing; they do nothing with the knowledge they receive.

*But be **doers of the word**, and not hearers only...*

James 1:22
(Emphasis mine)

You are going to take truths from the Word of God and, as you "hear" them, you will also begin to "work" them, acting on what you know to make it effective in your life. By this you will build spiritual muscles becoming stronger and stronger in your faith, enabling you to work powerfully and effectively in the Kingdom of God, resulting in a victorious life in Christ.

Knowing the rich fullness of God's Word hidden in these secrets is wonderful. Putting that truth into action is powerful! Your marriage will transform into a place of peace, protection and fulfillment. Your children will be grounded in the truth, not blown about with every wind of human philosophy and cunning of the devil. Just like Elisha, God's power will be unleashed to protect you from those who seek to destroy your work, your family, or your reputation.

If that sounds exciting to you, it is time to introduce you to your power stations. When you turn this page, you will step into the power zone where you will begin tapping into God's immeasurable greatness of power for your life.

ENDNOTES

[1] To hear examples of Marjorie teaching her children in their living room church time, visit the website at KingdomPurposeLife.com/living-room

[2] For additional help and next steps you can take in your home to prepare for God's power to flow in your life, check out the online video teaching course *"Welcome to Our Home, God"*

MarjorieLou.com/welcome-to-our-home-God

8 video sessions and printable worksheets

Why did I make this online course? Many people told me they wished I could come to their house, sit on their couch, and help them know what to do in their own homes so they can walk in the power of God. I personally would love to come to your home, and everyone else's too! But I am physically constrained for obvious reasons. This eCourse is the next best thing!

I come into your home via 8 videos with accompanying worksheets and other bonuses throughout. I personally help you prepare your household for the power of God to flow in your home, your family, and your life. I help you educate your family members. I assist you in exposing hindrances and traps the enemy may have set for you. I give you direction in moving forward and walking in that immeasurable greatness of power God promises to those who believe. *Marjorie*

Regular price $59.
Your discounted price ONLY $29!
That's 50% off!
Register Now at
MarjorieLou.com/welcome-to-our-home-God

Chapter 7

Secret Number Four

Get in the Word

You have now learned three secrets that have prepared your heart and your mind for containing and properly handling the power of God. Your eyes are beginning to open to the Kingdom of God. In secret number one, you learned the source of His vast power, as you learned how to see past the natural world and begin getting glimpses of the supernatural by shifting your paradigm. You discovered the importance of keeping your mind and heart focused on Jesus Christ so that through Him, you can overcome the circumstances in your life.

Secret number two handed you a keyring with three critical keys to preparing your heart to receive the power of God. Victorious Christians always remember human power fails, because it is Jesus himself that performs miracles through your hands. No human can do such in and of themselves. You must put your faith in God's Word in every situation you face, no matter how dire or impossible, if you want to see His promises manifest in your life.

Secret number three revealed a common thread that runs through the lives of all powerful Christians. These people view God as their life source, not a weekly scheduled event.

They keep Jesus ever before their eyes through singing, praying, fasting, and reading their Bibles daily. They spend blocks of time alone with God, quiet in His presence, to lift Him up and listen for His voice. They introduce their children into such disciplines as they explain the importance of this sacrifice of time.

Now that your heart and mind are prepared to receive the power, it is time to build your spiritual muscles so you are capable of grabbing hold of and utilizing that power. To do this, you must get to know your power stations. Each station is a crucial step to gaining God's power. The more you exercise your spiritual muscles at these secret stations, the more powerful a Christian you become. It is time to get excited, because God is excited over you! He longs to see you take the power He made available to you and flex your spiritual muscles for His glory. I am excited for you because I know He will begin today introducing you to His magnificent power. This is the beginning of the abundant life Jesus came to give to you. Are you ready to take that gift and make Him proud?

Secret Number Four

Power Station #1
You must abide in the Word of God

The most crucial aspect of a powerful life in the Kingdom of God is to

Get in the Word!
Stay in the Word!
Live in the Word!

Before you start thinking, "What! I've heard that before. That's not a secret!" let me remind you that we have shifted your paradigm to a Kingdom mindset where much is happening behind the scenes (the part you cannot perceive with your five senses) in multiple dimensions where your only functional eyes are your faith in God's Word. If you get in the Word here in the natural world, much will be happening on your behalf in the supernatural. Getting in the Word is like setting the squelch on your walkie talkie and tuning your frequency to God's channel so you can safely and successfully tread through the minefield of life.

There are hundreds of reasons to get in the Word and stay in the Word. Primarily, the Bible reveals who Jesus is, what He came to accomplish on your behalf, and how your life should be lived in response to Him. The answer to every life question can be found in those powerful pages. I want to give you four primary reasons to get in the Word as it relates to becoming a powerful Christian.

Reason 1 - The Word is Jesus

The most obvious way to get in the Word is through reading the Bible. I'll discuss many ways you can do this later in this chapter. Getting in the Word; however, entails much more than just reading your Bible every day.

I revealed in Chapter Four that Jesus is the Word of God made manifest into human form and Who dwelt among men. Now that He has left his earthly body and returned to the right hand of the Father, it does not mean He is unavailable to have a relationship with us. To the contrary, He is more available because He is no longer limited to earthly confines.

Thousands thronged Him as He walked this earth in Human form. Few could get up close to him. Very few of those who sought him had any relationship with him.

Now, seated at the right hand of the Father, He has shed His fleshly tent and is available to all who seek Him. Somehow, in those dimensions we cannot understand, he is able to manifest to all, save everyone, help those who seek Him, and enjoy relationship with anyone who chooses to abide in Him.

"Abide in me, and I in you.
As the branch cannot bear fruit by itself, unless it abides in the vine,
neither can you, unless you abide in me."

John 15:4

****

"And now, little children, abide in him,
so that when he appears we may have confidence
and not shrink from him in shame
at his coming."

1 John 2:28

****

"I am the vine; you are the branches.
Whoever abides in me and I in him,
he it is that bears much fruit,
for apart from me you can do nothing."

John 15:5

These are but a few of the passages that talk about abiding in Jesus. When spending time in these passages, I used to ask of God, "I want to abide in You. But how do I do that, exactly?"

It is hard for me to imagine spoken words becoming a person. That is because I am thinking in natural earthly terms. If I could think in more than three dimensions, maybe I could grasp that God's spoken Word became flesh. I do not need to grasp it for it to be true. I must use my faith as my eyes and see that this is truth from God.

In the beginning was the Word,
and the Word was with God,
and the Word was God.
He was in the beginning with God.

John 1:1

Notice in the passage above the pronoun for "the Word" is *He*, and not *it*.

And the Word became flesh
and dwelt among us

John 1:14

If you want to abide in Jesus, then get into the Word, because He is the Word.

"If you abide in my word,
you are truly my disciples."

John 8:31

Now I understand that to abide in Jesus Christ is to abide in the Word of God. This does not mean simply reading a predesignated amount of the Book every day and proclaim, "There. I read my five chapters today. I have abided in the Word. Done."

I believe there is more to abiding in the Word.

> *Whoever keeps his commandments*
> *abides in God,*
> *and God in him.*
> *And by this we know that he abides in us,*
> *by the Spirit whom he has given us.*
>
> 1 John 3:24

****

> *No one who abides in him keeps on sinning;*
> *no one who keeps on sinning*
> *has either seen him or known him*
>
> 1 John 3:6

Abiding in the Word is not just reading the Word, it is living the Word. Every action, every decision, every response to every situation should be based on the Word of God. If you abide in that Word, if you abide in Jesus Christ, then you will know how to handle every situation that arises in your marriage, your parenting, your workplace, with your extended family members and with strangers on the street.

> *"I came that they may have life*
> *and have it abundantly."*
>
> John 10:10

Jesus is your life, so abiding in Him is abiding in your life source. His Kingdom is your power source, so abiding in His Kingdom is abiding in your power source. Outside of Jesus Christ, there is no life nor power. Getting into the Word is getting into your source of life and power.

Reason 2 - The Word is Alive

Since Jesus is alive, the Word of God is alive.

> *For the word of God is living and active,*
> *sharper than any two-edged sword,*
> *piercing to the division of soul and of spirit,*
> *of joints and of marrow,*
> *and discerning the thoughts and intentions of the heart.*
>
> Hebrews 4:12

The Word of God is not just a book. It is Jesus Christ Himself and it is alive, because He is alive. Only Jesus can discern the thoughts and intentions of the heart. No man is able.

There is something more this passage reveals about the Word of God. We learn the Word divides soul and spirit. Most people do not realize they have a soul and a spirit, nevertheless realize the need to have them divided. If you ask most Christians, they will say that the soul and the spirit are the same. Let's look at soul and spirit for a minute and see how they are different and why they need to be divided.

Now may the God of peace himself sanctify you completely, and may your whole spirit and soul and body be kept blameless at the coming of our Lord Jesus Christ.

1 Thessalonians 5:23

In this passage, Paul refers to your spirit, soul and body. He clearly defines three parts to us. I love this because it reveals yet another way we are made in the image of God. He consists of three parts: Father, Son and Holy Spirit. We consist of three parts: spirit, soul and body.

Most Christians know what their body is. We live with that part every day. We see it in the mirror's reflection. We feed it, tend its needs and provide it comfort. We feel it in the form of pain, hunger, thirst, sleepiness, cold or heat. Most people would say, that's the "me" part of me. Certainly, it is the three-dimensional physical part of me that we know the most about.

The soul is the part of you usually associated with your mind. Your thoughts, feelings, and emotions are a part of your soul, as is your intellect, reasoning, and logic. You think and feel with your soul. You cannot see your soul, but you are in touch with it every day since your emotions and thinking let themselves be known to you all day long. This is where you feel sad, grief, happy, excited, annoyed, angry or content. You are constantly analyzing, comparing, judging, solving, and pondering.

The spirit is the inner part of you. Paul refers to it as your inner being in Ephesians 3:16 and Romans 7:22. He refers to it as the inner self in 2 Corinthians 4:16. This is the part of you that was dead before you knew Christ but was made alive by the Holy Spirit when you were saved by Him. You are not in touch with it in the natural. You cannot feel it or discern it with your natural senses in a tangible way.

Jesus answered him, "Truly, truly, I say to you, unless one is born again he cannot see the kingdom of God." Nicodemus said to him, "How can a man be born when he is old? Can he enter a second time into his mother's womb and be born?" Jesus answered, "Truly, truly, I say to you, unless one is born of water and the Spirit, he cannot enter the kingdom of God. That which is born of the flesh is flesh, and that which is born of the Spirit is spirit."

John 3:3-6

You must be born of the Spirit to belong to Jesus. This is referred to as being "born again." The spirit of man died at the fall of man in the garden of Eden. Man's dead spirit is made alive again at salvation.

Your spirit is where God's Spirit connects with you and communicates with you. It is by the Spirit that the Holy Spirit leads you into all truth,[1] brings scriptures to your remembrance,[2] and interprets spiritual things to you.[3]

The flesh operates in the natural realm. The spirit does not, for it operates in the supernatural realm, in those additional dimensions you cannot discern with your five senses. The Holy Spirit operates in the supernatural realm also.

If God is trying to tell me something or lead me into all truth and at the same time I am having my own thoughts of all kinds, and additionally the enemy is trying to affect my mind, how am I supposed to know when it is God talking to me, the enemy is trying to sway me, or I am just having my own brainy thoughts?

> *For the word of God is living and active,*
> *sharper than any two-edged sword,*
> *piercing to the division of soul and of spirit*
>
> *Hebrews 4:12*

Since you cannot tell the difference between your soul and your spirit, you must have the Word of God divide it for you. There is no other way to tell the difference between hearing God's voice or hearing your own thoughts. It is only by the Word of God that you can experience this division of your soul and spirit, whereby you can begin to discern between the two. No human effort will do the job. It is not a matter of the will, but of the Word.

You are supposed to be led by the Spirit. If your soul and spirit are not divided you can easily think it is God leading you, when you are really being led by your own self. The scariest part about that is you think it is God leading you when it is yourself. You have lost the squelch on your walkie talkie and accidentally tuned into a channel that cannot help you and will probably lead you to step on some landmines.

You can only serve one master. According to Romans 10, we are to proclaim Jesus as our master. He is our Lord. He is the authority under which we voluntarily place ourselves. Most Christians would say they have done just that. It is, after all, this confession that leads to our salvation.

> *If you confess with your mouth that Jesus is Lord
> and believe in your heart that
> God raised him from the dead,
> you will be saved.*
>
> Romans 10:9

Jesus Christ is our one master. Or is He?

What happens when your soul screams out to you with all its emotions flaring?

> "Tell that person how wrong they are!"
> "How dare they say that about me!"
> "I am so insulted by those words!"
> "How dare you!"

When this happens, your soul is demanding you do something about the situation.

> "Go tell your friends what they did to you."
> "Make sure you humiliate that person for embarrassing you."
> "Fire back harsh words to set that jerk straight."
> "Make him look bad in front of the boss."
> "Show her how smart you really are."

Wait a minute. Jesus said to:

Love your enemies	Matthew 5:44
Do good to those who hate you	Luke 6:27
Bless those who curse you	Luke 6:28
Pray for those who persecute you	Matthew 5:44

Your emotions demand one response while Jesus commands another. Now you are faced with a choice, and how you respond to this choice will determine who your master really is. Do you obey your emotions? Or do you obey Jesus Christ? If you obey your emotions, then your soul is your master. If you obey Jesus, then Jesus is your master. You cannot serve two masters, especially when they are telling you to have totally opposite responses to your situation. You will choose to obey one or the other.

You may now be thinking, "I can't help how I feel. God made me this way. How can He expect me to do any different from how I feel?" By thinking this way, you are essentially proclaiming that your emotions must be obeyed because God gave you those emotions and that's who you really are. This is because you have not yet experienced division of soul and spirit. Yes, the emotions are real. But they are not in their proper place. God blessed you with emotions to be your helper, to make you aware of things and be able to assess situations. Yet God never intended for your emotions to control or rule over you.

It may seem Jesus' command is impossible. Love my enemies? I can love my friends and family easily enough, but my enemies? Jesus did not command you to do something He cannot empower you to accomplish. God knows what happens behind that veil when you are kind to those who mistreat you. When the Holy Spirit is leading you, He will not have you retaliate or set some jerk straight. He will always lead you to esteem others higher than yourself [4] and to lay down your life (passions and desires) for others. Remember the landmines. Obeying God instead of your emotions is like crawling in a shelter of protection where the enemy's weapons cannot hurt you. Obeying your emotions will lead you to explosion after explosion because emotions are in the natural realm where Satan has his domain for now with all his destructive weapons.

Could this be the cause of your problems today?

Do Not Despair

Begin today looking for those moments when you face such decisions, then notice whether you obeyed your emotions or the Word. It will take practice, so do not be discouraged when you catch yourself giving in to the pressure of your emotions. Your emotions have been bossing you around for a long time and must be tamed. If you stay in the Word, you will eventually begin to respond to situations according to the Word. That first time you obey the Word and refrain from following your emotions, you will rejoice in your spirit! It will be one of the highlights of your life, because it will mark a breakthrough of freedom from the bondage of the captivity of your mind and the beginning of true victory in Jesus Christ! Congratulations! Your soul and spirit are dividing! You have felt your first taste of God's power in you!

Any time you feel like you failed again, remember, Your Father in heaven is beside you, cheering you on. He, like an earthly father with his child, wants more than anything to see you, His child, walking in the victory He provided for you through the sacrifice of His Son. His Spirit is always with you, ready to assist you, leading you to scriptures and helping you to resist the tantrums of your soul so you can choose obedience to the Word.

You need to be in the Word of God until you reach the point the Word divides your soul and spirit. If all you learned from this book was about your need for division of soul and spirit and put that teaching into practice until you achieved it, it will be worth exceedingly far more than you paid for this publication. For your Spirit to be made alive and then divided from the soul may be one of the most powerful aspects of the Word and one of the most glorious achievements Jesus accomplished in His earthly tenure. When that happens, you gain the ability to hear the voice of God clearly and follow His voice no matter what your emotions are screaming at you. It is like being catapulted through a threshold of power in the Kingdom of God. This is one reason why Satan attacks every attempt you make to commit to spending time in God's Word, and why he keeps your emotions flaring. Have you noticed Satan does this to you? Now you understand why. Do not let him use your emotions as a weapon against you or keep you from the freedom found only in Jesus Christ.

Reason 3 - The Word Renews the Mind

Therefore, if anyone is in Christ, he is a new creation. The old has passed away; behold, the new has come.

2 Corinthians 5:17

Marvelous mysteries happen beyond that veil in those other dimensions we cannot perceive. You experience a change as your old human nature is exchanged for a new Godly nature.

Once you become a new creation in Christ, does that mean you are all brand new and old habits disappear automatically? That would be great if, when you put off the old man, old habits disappeared and new mannerisms and mindsets were automatically put in place. If you have been born again as a new creation, why is transformation not so instantaneous as this?

It is true you and I have been translated from the old kingdom of darkness and now walk in His marvelous Kingdom.[5] But during our captivity by the enemy we were subjected to a system of brainwashing where we were taught lies and believed them as truth.

> *...seeing that you have put off the old self with its practices and have put on the new self, which is being renewed in knowledge after the image of its creator.*
>
> *Colossians 3:9-10*

Just before this verse, Paul labels the practices of the old self referring to some of them as "what is earthly in you" (verses 5-8). Then he makes this statement quoted above (verses 9-10) before going on to tell us the practices we must now put on (verses 12-17). Why did Paul feel the need to insert this passage between our old practices and our new ones?

Paul teaches us that even though we have been made a new creation, the mind is still used to all the old ways in which we once walked. To walk in the new behaviors of the new self we must have our minds renewed in knowledge, (in other words we must have our minds renewed in the Word of God), so that the transformation process can be completed, making us in the likeness of Jesus Christ. In order to walk in the new practices that Paul teaches us to "put on," we must be in the Word, being renewed by the Word. Romans 12:2 shows us that transformation is performed by the renewal of the mind. Through the Word we are renewed into the image of Christ[6] and we have the mind of Christ.[7]

> *Do not be conformed to this world, but be transformed by the renewal of your mind...*
>
> *Romans 12:2*

In volume 1 of my Renewing the Mind Series, entitled *Miracles and Healings*, I shared information I learned from a missionary who works with human trafficking. I wrote:

> *It is a common occurrence with victims rescued out of captivity that they have to be "deprogrammed" and therefore require a period of time before they can return to normal society. I learned of this phenomena through a friend of mine, Mary Johnston, who was working with a ministry rescuing women out of sex slave trafficking. These women required one to two years and sometimes more just to get their minds renewed in the truth of their value as a person and the correct way to function in normalized societal situations before they would be ready to live freely.*
>
> *Since we have been rescued out of the hands of the enemy, Paul knew we must be renewed in truth in order to implement the deprogramming required to reverse the damage of the brainwashing we had been subjected to by the enemy during our internment. Without this critical step of being renewed in truth, we will not be able to function as a "new man" successfully utilizing our new nature. We instead continue in the old way of thinking and acting.*[8]

Very few Christians understand their need to renew their mind so that the world's way of thinking can be washed out of their system. Instead, many Christians continue to live by the world's thinking patterns, trying to somehow combine that with living by the Bible. Rarely will God's way and the world's way be the same. Conflict after conflict leaves the average Christian feeling like a dismal failure in their Christian walk. They are stepping on landmines but cannot figure out what they are doing wrong.

Getting into the Word and staying in the Word are the only ways to renew your mind into the likeness of Jesus Christ. It is the only way to wash the world out of your thinking. Once you have begun to deprogram from the world's thinking, you begin to think like Jesus thinks and act like Jesus acts. Then you will realize the demands of your emotions have less control over you. Through the power of the Word, you will break the strongholds the world seems to still have on you so that you may finally put off the old self with its practices. And you will experience the exhilarating freedom of walking in the new self after the image of your Creator.

Reason 4 - The Word is Your Weapon

Put on the whole armor of God,
that you may be able to stand against
the schemes of the devil.
For we do not wrestle against flesh and blood,
but against the rulers, against the authorities,
against the cosmic powers over this present darkness,
against the spiritual forces of evil in the heavenly places.

Ephesians 6:10-12

In this life, you fight an enemy you cannot see. No, your enemy is not that unfair boss of yours. Your enemy is the force that is behind that boss. Believe it or not, your boss is a victim, a prisoner of war, being used to do evil biddings. The spiritual forces of evil influencing your boss are your real enemy. This is one of the reasons Jesus told you to do good to those who mistreat you. People are not your real enemy.

How do you battle against cosmic powers and spiritual forces in heavenly places that you cannot even see? How are you to battle an enemy with that kind of advantage over you?

*Therefore take up the whole armor of God,
that you may be able to withstand in the evil day,
and having done all, to stand firm.
Stand therefore.... and take the...
sword of the Spirit,
which is the word of God*

Ephesians 6:13-14, 17

God has equipped you for the battle. The entire armor God supplied is a study all to itself, but for the purpose of this book, I want to focus on the weapon He has placed in your hand, the sword of the Spirit which is the Word of God.

We will learn all about how to use this weapon in the next chapter. For now, understand that speaking words has a tremendous effect in the supernatural. When you specifically speak the Words contained within your Bible, it is like super-charged ammunition to take down the enemy. God's Word is higher, with more authority than any other word in the universe. What God says happens.

Remember, God sees everything happening in all the dimensions, both natural and supernatural. Knowing exactly what you need, He provided His Word to be your weapon. When the enemy attacks you, fire at him with Gods Word spoken out of your mouth and you will stop his schemes in their tracks. You will be amazed to learn just how powerful this sword really is.

Getting in the Word and staying in the Word is like filling your ammunition bag before going on the battlefield. The Holy Spirit will prompt you to use specific scriptures for each attack. The more scriptures you hide in the ammunition bag called your heart, the more the Holy Spirit has to draw from when leading you through the battle. Your job is to grab hold of your weapon and load up with ammunition.

When an attack comes, there is nothing more critical for your protection than your weapon. With it, you can stop or deter the enemy from attacking and protect what is yours. But in order for your weapon to be a truly useful tool, you must know your weapon – backwards and forwards, inside and out.

New military recruits receive much training with their weapon in boot camp. They use it, clean it, take it apart, and reassemble it over and over and over again. With these exercises they get so familiar with their weapon, they can wield it in battle with no thought of it at all. They know it so well that it is almost like a part of them. When responding to orders, a soldier obeys, thinking only of the task at hand and not thinking, "How does this thing work?" or, "How do I load these bullets?" To flounder with your weapon while in battle is to endanger your life and the lives of your comrades.

A recruit who is not diligent in weapon training will be of no good use to his commanding officers. To the contrary, he will be a hindrance to higher authority as he will not be reliable to be called upon for missions and tasks.

You have been issued your weapon for battle. It is the sword of the Spirit, which is the Word of God. But what good is that weapon if you don't know how to use it? Like the soldier recruits, you must know your weapon. You need to work with it, break it down, understand it, and then aim it precisely at the enemy's forehead. Now, while in boot camp, is the safe time to store it up in the warehouse of your heart, and practice using it, shooting practice rounds (speaking it out until you are comfortable with it) and shooting it at the enemy (speaking it out when the enemy attacks) until you know your weapon without even thinking about it.

How to Get the Word in You

You now see how critical it is to get in the Word of God and stay there. It literally becomes your life, your breath, and your only hope.

There are many wonderful ways and techniques to help you build an arsenal of scripture in your heart. Below are a few of my favorites.

Traditional reading plans – This may involve topical studies, read the Bible in a year plans, or simply a commitment to reading a certain amount of scripture every day. This may be organized by topic, passages, chapters, books, or by setting timeframes such as one hour a day, or thirty minutes at each meal.

Many times, I take a passage and read it over and over until I know it got past my head as knowledge and it got down into my spirit as "knowing." Once, God set me on a program where I was to read all of Paul's letters in their chronological order. I read a whole book at the time, and I read each book fifty times before moving on to the next book. I had to use tally marks at the end of the books to keep track. At the end of this process, I had tons of notes of things I could have never put together without the repetition. Often it was the tenth to fifteenth reading of the book before the deeper meanings began to emerge for me. It was a long and arduous process, but tremendously exciting because of how much I learned from those letters.

Audio – Faith comes by hearing and hearing by the Word of God.[9] With today's technology, you can hear the Word any time at any place. Download or stream your Bible on your favorite mobile device. With earbuds, you can be anywhere filling yourself with God's Word without disturbing those around you. My husband puts earbuds in his tablet at night and falls asleep hearing the Word. This works at home, traveling, in crowded public spaces, virtually anywhere.

Meditation – I wrote a blog post entitled *Chewing the Cud* [10] where I described pulling up scriptures and chewing on them to extract all the truth out of them. I have spent a lot of time chewing on God's Word and some of my revelation of scripture meanings has come during those times. I remember them, repeat them to myself, and ask God questions about them. This is a method you can use anywhere. Not only have I used it during my quiet times with God, I have used it doing housework, exercising, waiting for appointments, and riding in a car, bus or airplane. Whether walking around the house, jogging through the neighborhood, or strolling through a park, museum or grocery store, you can find awesome times to pull up God's Word and chew on it.

Memory – Memorizing scriptures is a bit more traditional, but it is very powerful. This is the grit of getting your weapon razor sharp. It is wonderful to memorize word for word, but some scriptures I simply repeat the truth the scripture contains in my own vernacular. Often, I weave these scriptures into my daily language, whereby I have frequently spoken God's truth over someone who was averse to anything about God. Little did they know I had used my weapon in the supernatural realm over them. I constantly use my weapon, so I am ready at the slightest provocation from the enemy to pull it out and wield it skillfully.

Study – With today's mobile devices, studying the Word is easier than ever. My home library is filled with volumes of large print books that were once required for deeper study. Now I carry most of those volumes on my phone or tablet. With a simple click I can see the original Greek or Hebrew words and their definitions. I can pull from commentaries or history books in a flash.

However you decide to get in the Word, just get in and stay there. Abide in Jesus until you are transformed into His likeness and experience the division of soul and spirit. Start noticing when you must decide between responding to your emotions or obeying the Word of God. Let the Word renew your mind into the image of your creator.[11] Then wield your weapon at the cosmic powers set out to destroy you and your family. You cannot see your enemy, but God can, so take your Sword of the Spirit and listen for His voice, follow what he says, and watch your enemy flee. With the Word of God deeply entrenched in your spirit, you will walk in God's power in your life.

With your new eyes that can see beyond the natural world and three critical keys in your pocket, you have begun to join the common thread of Christians who prioritize time with God. You have begun working out at secret power stations building spiritual muscles whereby you will do amazing deeds with God's power to bring glory to His Name.

Now that you have worked out at your first secret power station, do you feel excitement over what you are learning? That is likely your spirit rejoicing with His truth. The Holy Spirit wants you filled with His Word. The more you put inside, the more He has to work with when leading you into Kingdom opportunities or avoiding treacherous perils.

It is time to visit the second secret power station and begin working another spiritual muscle group. The next secret I reveal is one of the most important keys to experiencing God's power and where you will begin handling that power yourself. Beware! It is also one of the biggest hinderances you face to receiving that power.

ENDNOTES

[1] John 16:13 When the Spirit of truth comes, he will guide you into all the truth, for he will not speak on his own authority, but whatever he hears he will speak, and he will declare to you the things that are to come.

[2] John 14:26 But the Helper, the Holy Spirit, whom the Father will send in my name, he will teach you all things and bring to your remembrance all that I have said to you.

[3] 1 Corinthians 2:13 And we impart this in words not taught by human wisdom but taught by the Spirit, interpreting spiritual truths to those who are spiritual.

[4] Philippians 2:3 Do nothing from selfish ambition or conceit, but in humility count others more significant than yourselves.

[5] Colossians 1:13 He has delivered us from the domain of darkness and transferred us to the kingdom of his beloved Son,

[6] Romans 8:29 For those whom he foreknew he also predestined to be conformed to the image of his Son, in order that he might be the firstborn among many brothers.

[7] 1 Corinthians 2:16 "For who has understood the mind of the Lord so as to instruct him?" But we have the mind of Christ.

[8] Miracles and Healings, Renewing the Mind Series, Volume 1, © 2017, Marjorie Lou Ministries

[9] Romans 10:17 So faith comes from hearing, and hearing through the word of Christ.

[10] KingdomPurposeLife.com/cud

[11] Colossians 3:10 and have put on the new self, which is being renewed in knowledge after the image of its creator.

Chapter 8

Secret Number Five

The Spoken Word

You are well on your way to experiencing the power of God in your everyday life. You readied your heart to receive God's power by placing your three keys in your pocket. You disciplined your mind so it can function in that power, by spending much time in the Word and in God's presence. You understand the Word will be of no effect unless you act on what you hear.

You are now on a quest to build spiritual muscles so you will be fully equipped to do any work your King requires of you. The promises of God rest in His power, and He has made that power available to you for the provision and protection of your family, for the work of reaching the lost, and for other activities of the church as Jesus described, such as healing the sick, casting out demons and raising the dead.[1] Excitement builds as you slowly realize how these kinds of miracles will affect your family. Hope for your future grows because you are now realizing the promises of God are within your reach. If you keep moving forward and don't give up, you will soon grasp your first experience in God's power.

In the previous chapter, I introduced you to the first secret power station in the Kingdom of God. Getting into God's

Word has a whole new deeper meaning for you now. God's Word is alive and is your only true life source. It divides soul and spirit enabling you to clearly hear God's voice and distinguish it from your own thoughts or ideas. Your emotions have lost their long-standing control over you as you train yourself to obey God's Word rather than their rigorous demands.

The time has come to visit the next secret power station. This secret will reveal one of the most prominent factors in becoming a powerful Christian. With it, you will take your first steps in experiencing God's power. It is time to step out and take hold of the power in your own hands.

Secret Number Five

Power Station #2
There is tremendous power
in every word you speak

Spoken words are a major key to walking in the supernatural. At the same time, spoken words are the biggest hindrance against walking in that power.

Do you remember the old ditty your mother would tell you when the kids at school teased you?

Sticks and stones
may break my bones
but words will never harm me.

Mom meant well; however, I challenge that old cliché, because I have seen more damage done in the lives of people by words than stones could ever do. Bumps and bruises heal within days or weeks. Injuries incurred by words may remain raw decades after being spoken.

I would venture to say that most people don't think about words very often. The mouth opens and out flows every thought from your brain with no consideration of them being dangerous projectiles more damaging than flying stones. Some injuries from a spoken word never heal over an entire lifetime.

Yes, words are powerful. I want to show you why you must consider the critical importance of your words and why they are so powerful.

I have set before you life and death,
blessing and curse
... choose life

Deuteronomy 30:19

God is making a powerful statement in this passage of scripture. He says He places before mankind two choices, that of life and that of death. Then God adds something I considered rather strange. He tells us to choose life. Doesn't that seem like a no-brainer? Who would not automatically choose life? Is there anyone who would purposely choose death? Why would God need to tell you what to choose when the answer seems so obvious?

God told you what to choose because He knew you would need great encouragement in the process of choosing life. The way you choose life will go against everything in your human nature. It will not come effortlessly, and you will easily be deceived when making this crucial life or death choice. How is this choice made?

*Death and life
are in the power of the tongue*

Proverbs 18:21

Your tongue holds the power of choosing life or choosing death. When you open your mouth to speak and words flow, you are literally making a choice between life (God's Word and God's way, speaking blessing and operating in love) or you are choosing death (Satan's way, speaking evil, selfishness and hate). The choice between life and death is not a single moment in time when you pick one and call it done. The choice between life and death is a daily choice made repeatedly with every word that proceeds from your mouth. In the supernatural beyond that veil of perception, much happens depending on the choice you make.

In the Beginning

God revealed the power of the spoken word from the beginning. For six days the book of Genesis records "and God said" as He spoke everything into exitance. Other books of the Bible confirm that God created by speaking words.

the universe was created by the word of God

Hebrews 11:3

> *Let them praise the name of the Lord!*
> *For he commanded and they were created.*
>
> *Psalms 148:5*

David Spoke the Word

David speaks often of meditating on the Word of God.

> *but his delight is in the law of the Lord,*
> *and on his law he meditates day and night.*
>
> *Psalm 1:2*

In the English language, the word meditate means to have quiet moments of introspection or to engage in thought or contemplation. Basically, we think the word meditate means sitting and quietly thinking about a particular thing with all other thoughts excluded. It is rooted in the Hindu technique of acquiring a relaxed state by clearing the mind and chanting a mantra.

The Hebrew word translated meditate is "hagah." By definition, this Hebrew word does include times of thinking as in Proverbs 15:28 where the Bible says, "The heart of the righteous ponders how to answer." Here the word translated ponder is the Hebrew word hagah. The proverb essentially means a righteous man thinks before he speaks. But the definition of the word hagah reflects much more about speaking out loud than it does about thinking. According to Blue Letter Bible, the word means to growl, to utter, to mutter and to speak, as well as to mediate or imagine. When David spoke of meditating on the law day and night, he could have meant speaking it as well as thinking about it. With a look at scripture, I am certain at a minimum he meant both.

> *This Book of the Law shall not depart from your mouth,*
> *but you shall meditate on it day and night,*
> *so that you may be careful to do according to all that is written in it.*
> *For then you will make your way prosperous,*
> *and then you will have good success.*
>
> *Joshua 1:8*

Do you notice the Book of the Law should not depart from your mouth? The mouth is what you use to speak, not think. Therefore, when the passage goes on to say you shall meditate (hagah) it day and night, it is referring to the mouth, or to speaking. From this one verse alone we see tremendous benefits for speaking out the Word of God day and night.

I hagah the Word of God day and night. I mutter, utter or speak the Word wherever I am. When working around the house, walking, driving, or lying in bed just before sleep sets in, I am uttering the truths of God. To mutter is too imply speaking just above a whisper, more as to oneself. You can mutter anywhere without raising eyebrows.

When I first started to hagah the Word day and night, my children did raise an eyebrow. They wondered why Mom was talking to herself all the time. I explained to them what I had discovered, and they soon became used to it. Now it is normal life for them to hear me walking down the hall with a laundry basket in my hands speaking out the truths of God. Since I see no need to hold it to a "mutter" at home, they are hearing everything I say. Faith comes by hearing[2] so as they hear me speak it out, the faith of everyone in the home is building.

Once I understood the power of hagah, my life changed dramatically. It truly opened the doorway to the power of God pouring forth in my life. Because I speak out the Word all the time, you can bet it has penetrated my heart. Since my heart is so full of the Word, I think on it always. Therefore, I am truly doing hagah in the fullest sense. I speak it, think on it and imagine it day and night. This keeps me built up, strong, and focused on God at all times. It is renewing my mind to be in the likeness of Jesus Christ.

Your Weapon

In the last chapter you learned that the Word of God is your weapon against the enemy. It provides the only effective means of protection or defense against the enemy. You learned that getting into and staying in the Word is like filling your bag with super-charged ammunition for the battles.

You also learned that time in the Word is your practice with your weapon. Speaking it out under your breath day and night gives you ample opportunity to get comfortable with your weapon. When you read it, study it, and speak it out, it is like the soldier at boot camp learning to break down, clean, assemble, and shoot their weapon with accuracy.

When you practice hagah of the Word, you will be prepared to use your weapon when a situation requires it. The words flow as you aim your weapon straight at the heart of the enemy. You do not have to think about the weapon because you know your weapon well. You only need to keep your ear to your walkie talkie, let the Holy Spirit choose the bullet, and fire. Under these conditions, the enemy is hit full force with deadly accuracy. The enemy's schemes against you or your household are stopped cold.

Remember, only God sees what is really going on in all the dimensions of reality. Your job is to practice with your weapon and be ready. When you find yourself on the battlefield, you do what He says. You *say* what He says. And the Word of His power[3] will do all the work. It is just like shooting a gun. You hold the gun, point the gun, and pull the trigger, but it is the bullet that gets the job done. You speak those words and the sword of the Spirit slices the enemy to the core.

Jesus Taught Us How to Use Our Sword

Jesus Himself taught us this very lesson.

> *"Truly, I say to you, whoever says to this mountain,*
> *'Be taken up and thrown into the sea,'*
> *and does not doubt in his heart,*
> *but believes that what he says will come to pass,*
> *it will be done for him."*
>
> Mark 11:23

Do you have any mountains in your life? Jesus says to speak to the mountain and tell it to be thrown out! As one preacher put it, Jesus did not tell us to speak to God and tell Him all about our mountain. Jesus tells us to speak to that mountain and tell it all about our God! Tell that mountain in your life what God says, because God's Word is truth and power. When you do this, you are using God's immeasurable greatness of power to do far more abundantly than you can think or imagine according to the power at work in you, just as we discussed in chapter three. Jesus shows you that faith is released in what you say.

To see this in action, look at Acts chapter 3. Peter and John encountered a man lame from birth who regularly begged at the one of the temple gates. When this lame man asked Peter and John for money, Peter's response reveals He understood what Jesus was teaching.

> *"I have no silver and gold, but what I do have I give to you. In the name of Jesus Christ of Nazareth, rise up and walk!" And he took him by the right hand and raised him up, and immediately his feet and ankles were made strong. And leaping up, he stood and began to walk, and entered the temple with them, walking and leaping and praising God.*
>
> *Acts 3:6-8*

If most Christians encountered such a situation, we would be prone to grab the man by the hands and pray, "Dear God, please heal this lame man. Please make his feet and ankles strong." We would be talking to God about the mountain in this man's life. This is not at all what Peter prayed. Peter knew what Jesus taught because Peter was right there when Jesus taught about speaking to mountains. Therefore, Peter did not pray to God asking Him to do something. Instead Peter did something. He spoke according to what Jesus had taught him, his faith was released by what he said, and the man was instantly healed.

The same Spirit that raised Christ Jesus from the dead was on the inside of Peter. That is a lot of power inside of Peter. If you have the same Spirit inside of you, then He is inside you with all His immeasurable greatness of power, all available for you. All you need to do is speak His words and release His power to work through your life.

Who Jesus Addresses

Some may suggest that since Peter was an Apostle, he was able to perform miracles, and rightly so; however, the Apostles are not the only ones Jesus expects to speak out miracles. Take a look at His own words.

> *"Truly, I say to you,*
> *whoever says to this mountain,*
> *'Be taken up and thrown into the sea,'"*
>
> *Mark 11:23*

According to Jesus, the ones who will experience miracles is "whoever says." He did not limit it to the twelve disciples. He did not confine it to only leaders and pastors. He tells us that whoever speaks to the mountain will see the power of God in their lives.

Again, Jesus speaks just before He ascends to heaven to be at the right hand of the Father. He is departing this physical world to join again with the Father. These were to be His last words as a human. Jesus knew these would be extremely important words. What were the last words He spoke?

> *And these signs will accompany those who believe:*
> *in my name they will cast out demons;*
> *they will speak in new tongues;*
> *they will pick up serpents with their hands;*

and if they drink any deadly poison, it will not hurt them; they will lay their hands on the sick, and they will recover."

Mark 16:17-18

Jesus listed some miraculous feats as He spoke His last words. He was speaking directly to his disciples, but were the disciples the only ones He was addressing? Pay attention to who Jesus references.

And these signs will accompany those who believe

Jesus is referring to anyone who believes. I believe. Do you believe? If you answered yes, then Jesus is expecting you to speak, expecting the supernatural to work through your life.

Natural or Supernatural

What you speak is what you will get. Every time you speak, your spoken word aligns with the world or with God's Word. Every time you speak, you shoot missiles of destruction launched by Satan for his purposes, or you launch attacks against Satan to stop his evil works, all determined by the choice of your words.

You can only serve one master. You will speak according to what your emotions demand or you will speak according to what Jesus commands. The natural response is to obey your emotions. Be careful if you concede to those feelings, because they can be oh so deceitful. It seems like the fair thing, to retaliate against someone who has done you wrong so you can look good to others, but your feelings will never lead you to anything but selfishness and self-preservation. In the end you find yourself serving under a harsh task master who will burden you with his torturous load. You are living in the natural on Satan's turf, ignoring the other side of the veil. You have turned off your walkie talkie. You are sinking in a sea of circumstances that control your life.

If you choose to serve Jesus Christ, He will lead you to lay it all down and not worry about what others think about you. When He tells you to do good to those who mistreat you, He knows both sides of the veil. Trust Him, obey Him, and all the power of heaven is released on your behalf for both provision and protection for your circumstance. Every one of Satan's landmines lay dormant. It may go against every natural thing you see or feel, but you are not living by your natural eyes. You listen to your walkie talkie. You are choosing to live by faith with your eyes fixed on Jesus. Jesus' burden is light because He is doing all the work. You are walking on top of the sea of your circumstances and it is not sucking you down.

Once, in the corridors of a church we attended years ago, I was berated by another lady from the church. With hands on hips, she yelled at me, scolding me for things that were not true or accurate. Being fairly articulate, I could have easily turned on her, and responded back with words that would have made her shrink in shame and humiliation.

If I had obeyed my emotions and acted according to the natural, I would have chosen words of death, releasing destructive missiles straight at her heart. Satan would have thrown a party in celebration for all the damage I would have done to one of God's precious ones.

Instead, I let the Spirit of God lead me, speak through me, and handle the situation. I chose life by responding in the supernatural. My first thought was not concern for justifying myself and setting her straight. My first thought was concern for her, wondering what would have made her so angry. I saw her as captured by an enemy who was messing with her emotions by telling her lies to stir up death and destruction.

I returned to her a soft answer. I did not tell her how wrong she was. Instead, I apologized for whatever I could have possibly done to make her so angry. My soft answer was met with further fury, to which I responded softly once more. I continued with this for three rounds of anger, then finally this lady realized I was not going to engage and began to calm down. At that point we could converse about her concerns and work through the problem.

Her emotions were real. She was angry, and I was the target. But my response to the situation is what determined the outcome. I responded according to what the word says.

*A soft answer turns away wrath,
but a harsh word stirs up anger.*

Proverbs 15:1

The result? The anger was turned away and a relationship was salvaged with minimal damage.

Will you serve Satan by speaking what your emotions are raging resulting in evil, selfishness and ultimately death? Or will you serve God by speaking out His words of truth no matter how the situation looks to you in the natural, resulting in life, victory and freedom? Death and life are truly in the power of the tongue. You will serve only one master, and the choice between masters is made in the words you speak.

It really comes down to this simple but challenging question. Do you trust God more than you trust your own feelings?

Handle With Care

Now you are beginning to understand the power of words. Every word that proceeds out of your mouth is like having a weapon in your hand. Like any weapon, they can be utilized for protection of the innocent or destruction of your adversary. Like any weapon, they must be handled with utmost care.

Your Weapon is Pointing at Others

You think you are just telling how you feel. You simply react to a frustrating child or an unfair boss. Little did you know that you were pointing a weapon at their heart and shooting lethal ammunition.

Now it is becoming clearer as to why Jesus said:

> *"I tell you, on the day of judgment people will give account for every careless word they speak,"*
>
> *Matthew 12:36*

Just like any soldier, you will account for every time you fired your weapon. Each time you open your mouth, you are responsible for what flows out of it, because with every word comes blessing or cursing, life or death. Your adversary is spiritual and not natural. Every word must fall in line with God's Word for you to hit your target. The wrong words end up moving the sights of your weapon to a human target. If you pull the trigger, Satan has just taken a shot at one for whom Christ died[4] and you are his trigger man.

> *"But I say to you who hear,*
> *Love your enemies,*
> *do good to those who hate you,*
> *bless those who curse you,*
> *pray for those who abuse you.*
> *To one who strikes you on the cheek,*
> *offer the other also,*
> *and from one who takes away your cloak*
> *do not withhold your tunic either.*
> *Give to everyone who begs from you,*
> *and from one who takes away your goods*
> *do not demand them back.*
> *And as you wish that others would do to you,*
> *do so to them."*
>
> Luke 6:27-31

Do you find these words as challenging as I do? They seem impossible to me. What human can do these things and have a pure heart about it? Consider these words were spoken by Jesus Himself. Is Jesus asking you and me to do something impossible to accomplish?

> *Jesus looked at them and said,*
> *"With man it is impossible, but not with God.*
> *For all things are possible with God."*
>
> Mark 10:27

The only reason it seems impossible to accomplish is because you are looking at it from a human standpoint. Humanly, all these things are impossible because all human efforts ultimately fail. Only in Jesus Christ can you walk out these commands. Only when you are so desperate to listen to your walkie talkie can the impossible be done, because you know behind that veil, there is something that happens on your behalf when you lay down your life and follow Jesus. Only Jesus can lead you away from the dangers of the landmines.

Paul challenges us in an interesting way as he discusses believers suing other believers in the city of Corinth.

> *but brother goes to law against brother,*
> *and that before unbelievers?*
> *To have lawsuits at all with one another*
> *is already a defeat for you.*
> *Why not rather suffer wrong?*
> *Why not rather be defrauded?*
> *But you yourselves wrong and defraud—*
> *even your own brothers!*
>
> 1 Corinthians 6:6-8

Paul is asking why these believers cannot simply accept that wrong has been done to them. He is asking, "What's the big deal. Can't you just let it go?" I ask you the same. If someone does you wrong, do you have to open your mouth and say whatever your emotions are screaming? Can you not rather accept it and not let it get to you? Can you trust God more than you trust your raging demanding feelings?

This is why Paul teaches:

> *...take every thought captive to obey Christ,*

2 Corinthians 10:5

We are to take every thought and test it against scripture before we open our mouth as a floodgate of unchecked evil. Every word that proceeds out of your mouth is either blessing or cursing, life or lethal. Your choice of words determines who's camp you are working for. Satan urges you to follow those emotions so he can gain an inroad to your life for destruction. Could this be why you have chaos in your life right now?

When you learn to have control over your words you shut the gate on the enemy. All of his schemes fail, because you avoid his landmines.

Your Weapon is Pointing at Yourself

The words you speak have just as much power over yourself as they do over others. How often does the enemy take your weapon and try to get you to commit spiritual suicide? Consider what words you speak to yourself, about yourself, that damage your walk with Christ.

> I'm not good enough
> I'm sick and tired of dealing with this problem
> I can't do that (even though the Word says to, such as love your enemy)
> I am so sick today
> I'm not good enough for God to love me
> Nobody likes me
> I'm so stupid sometimes

Words you speak over yourself can often be far deadlier than those others speak toward you. As one preacher once put it, most Christians are digging their own graves with their tongues. God sent Jesus to set you free from the dominion of sin. He came to give you life abundantly. He came to set you free from the hand of the enemy. In His hand are victory and freedom. When you speak words of death or defeat, you are speaking against the truth of God's Word. Again, you are not to speak what your feelings demand. They are deceptive. You are to speak what the Word of God says about you.

...we have the mind of Christ.

1 Corinthians 2:16

****

Therefore, if anyone is in Christ, he is a new creation. The old has passed away; behold, the new has come.

2 Corinthians 5:17

****

For sin will have no dominion over you,...

Romans 6:14

****

And the Lord will make you the head and not the tail, and you shall only go up and not down,...

Deuteronomy 28:13

****

by whose stripes you were healed.

1 Peter 2:24 (NKJV)

(The issue of sickness is huge in the body of Christ. I address it in detail in chapter 11.)

Even in jest, the words can still have power over your circumstances. For instance, something I used to say frequently for a giggle:

"That chocolate cake is to die for!"

No! It is not! I was having health issues and never considered that perhaps I was speaking death over myself! I began to take responsibility for every word I spoke. When I caught myself saying something that was contrary to what God says about me, I would immediately repent of it and speak the truth over it. For instance, I often commented how terrible my memory was getting. I catch myself saying (even if just in my mind), "I cannot remember anything anymore!" Once I realize what I have done, I speak out loud what God says about me. "I have the mind of Christ! I have the mind of Christ!" Once I began making these changes, I found I spoke such things less often and changes began to happen. Nothing was initiated in the natural. My health issues simply began diminishing for no natural reason. My memory improved. Energy returned. Something was taking place behind the veil, in the supernatural realm. My words spoken in God's truth released the power of God, and His promises in the Word began to manifest in my life.

I ask you to consider the words you are speaking over people in your life. If your children misbehave, do you let words of death slip out of your mouth? Have you called them stupid, crazy, or lazy? Then you should expect to see in them what you have spoken over them. Perhaps they are behaving that way, but speaking over them like that only insures nothing will change. It is better to replace your language with words that line up with God's Word.

For instance, if your child made a foolish decision, don't call him dumb. It would be better to say something like this, "Your decision doesn't seem like one a smart boy like you would make. What do you think a smart boy like you should have done?" You make the same point to the child, yet you speak over him what you expect to receive – a smart boy who makes good decisions. Before you scoff, remember, it will take more than one time speaking this way before the child begins to believe your words and produce those results. Trust that something is happening behind the veil in the supernatural realm and wait to see it come forth eventually in the natural. Speak words of life, and you will see life manifest.

I want you to consider how you speak in all of your relationships. Think about your spouse or your parents. How do you talk about those extended family members who are hard to deal with? How do you handle that troublesome neighbor? Has your boss or a coworker been challenging lately? Change your language, don't give up, and watch the power of the spoken word work in your life.

Paul once prayed for the Ephesians that the eyes of their understanding be opened. I pray for you that the eyes of your understanding are beginning to perceive the critical importance of your choice of words. They are not "just words." They not only damage more than sticks and stones, but are lethal affecting both this life and the one we will spend in eternity. Your ability to fulfill your destiny in Christ rests in the very crucial issue.

This secret power station requires a lot of heavy lifting. Be encouraged! No one is going to decide to change the way they speak and master it instantaneously. It will take time and practice. The payoff for your diligence will mean a victorious life in this world. Not only will your life change, but the destiny of your spouse and children will as well. Promises and protection will be in your right hand as the power of God proceeds from your mouth. Finally, your prayers will be answered when you use language that includes God's words spoken according to God's will.

Take a moment to savor the beauty of God's majesty and the power of His Word. Let him show you a picture of your life as you walk out all you are learning. That hope you are feeling is the truth of Jesus Christ and it will serve as a mighty anchor to hold you through any storm you face.[5]

Have you caught your breath?

Now that you understand the crucial importance of the words you speak, we will look at the times you speak according to the Word but feel like nothing happens. At the next secret power station, you will learn about a foundation that must under gird every word that comes out of your mouth. Without this foundation, the words you speak could lose their power, like a car trying to run on bad gasoline. You must build muscles in the next secret power station, so your words carry the power they were intended to produce.

ENDNOTES

[1]Matthew 10:8 Heal the sick, raise the dead, cleanse lepers, cast out demons. You received without paying; give without pay.

Mark 16:17-18 And these signs will accompany those who believe: in my name they will cast out demons; they will speak in new tongues; they will pick up serpents with their hands; and if they drink any deadly poison, it will not hurt them; they will lay their hands on the sick, and they will recover."

[2]Romans 10:17 So faith comes from hearing, and hearing through the word of Christ.

[3]Hebrews 1:3 He is the radiance of the glory of God and the exact imprint of his nature, and he upholds the universe by the word of his power. After making purification for sins, he sat down at the right hand of the Majesty on high,

[4]1 Corinthians 8:11 And so by your knowledge this weak person is destroyed, the brother for whom Christ died. Romans 14:15 For if your brother is grieved by what you eat, you are no longer walking in love. By what you eat, do not destroy the one for whom Christ died.

[5]Hebrews 6:19-20 We have this as a sure and steadfast anchor of the soul, a hope that enters into the inner place behind the curtain, where Jesus has gone as a forerunner on our behalf, having become a high priest forever after the order of Melchizedek.

Chapter 9

Secret Number Six

The Power of Believing

In the last chapter you learned the magnitude of the power behind every word you speak. You discovered the impact reaches beyond the veil of our natural world and directly effects happenings in the supernatural realm. By your choice of words, God's power is released on your behalf, or Satan's schemes explode in a myriad of trouble in your life.

There are times when you do speak what the Word says, but do not see the physical manifestation of that truth in the natural world. This is because you say things, but not necessarily believe what you say. What you say must be backed up by believing or you will not see what you say come to pass.

It is easier to have doubt than you might think. Doubt is simply believing the natural world over God's Word. Remember the brainwashing we talked about in chapter seven? You are brainwashed by a lifetime of responding to the natural world in natural ways. It is all you have known, and your mind is trained only to its ways.

Jesus knew this was a problem for mankind.

Therefore I tell you,
whatever you ask in prayer,
believe that you have received it,
and it will be yours.

Mark 11:24

****

And Jesus answered them,
"Truly, I say to you,
if you have faith and do not doubt,
you will not only do what has been done to the fig tree,
but even if you say to this mountain,
'Be taken up and thrown into the sea,'
it will happen."

Matthew 21:21

****

Jesus immediately reached out his hand
and took hold of him, saying to him,
"O you of little faith,
why did you doubt?"

Matthew 14:31
(When Peter was sinking when walking on the water)

> *Truly, I say to you, whoever says to this mountain,*
> *'Be taken up and thrown into the sea,'*
> *and does not doubt in his heart,*
> *but believes that what he says will come to pass,*
> *it will be done for him.*
>
> Mark 11:23

James adds his comments on doubting.

> *But let him ask in faith,*
> *with no doubting,*
> *for the one who doubts*
> *is like a wave of the sea that is driven and tossed by the wind.*
> *For that person must not suppose that he will receive*
> *anything from the Lord;*
> *he is a double-minded man,*
> *unstable in all his ways.*
>
> James 1:6-8

These are strong words spoken by both Jesus and James. I hope you are feeling how forceful they are in getting this vital information across to believers. Within these scriptures are secret number six of God's power and how to experience it in your life.

Secret Number Six

Power Station #3
You must believe God's Word until the believing gets past your head and down into your spirit.

Do You Believe Your Bible?

As Christians, most of us quickly attest that we believe the Bible. Since it is the infallible Word of God, we believe every word within is true. This was certainly my proclamation; however, like the rich young ruler,[1] God has His way of exposing the fallacy of what you *think* you believe.

Consider the following portions of scripture and ask yourself for each one, "Do I believe this is true?"

> A donkey spoke with human voice
> *(2 Peter 2:16 referring to Numbers 22:21-34)*
>
> The virgin shall conceive and bear a son
> *(Matthew 1:23)*
>
> Peter got out of the boat and walked on the water
> *(Matthew 14:29)*

What is your response to these verses? Do you believe these things to be true? Most all of us do believe them to be true. If it is in the Bible, I believe it! Simple as that!

A few problems arose for me in this area of believing. The first revealed itself during a family beach outing. As I stood by that ocean, the Lord questioned me, "Do you believe Peter walked on the sea?" I walked in the water's edge, noticing the total lack of resistance against my foot as I stepped in the surf's water again and again. I tried to imagine the water supporting my weight. Hmm. I believed it was true of Peter because the Bible says it happened. But at that moment of walking in the ocean's edge, I was forced to consider the physical nature of the question. A full-grown man, possibly two hundred pounds or more, stood on top of the water and it held his weight.

Brain Believing

When the Lord presents a question like that, He has a lesson in mind. He led me to understand that I had been believing with my head. It was human logic to conclude that, if the Bible says it, I am going to believe it. With my brain I was believing it based on a brain form of "knowing," or head knowledge.

If $a = b$ and $b = c$, then a must $= c$

To believe that a human being can get out of a boat and walk in the middle of a sea staying above the water from the ankles up – that was well beyond human believing or head knowledge. That takes a supernatural level of believing that only comes from the Spirit of God. It is a deeper level of "knowing" that only comes with full trust in God, resulting in full trust in the truth and power of His Word.

My second challenge in the area of believing happened over time as I watched several people who were strongly believing God would heal them from serious illness. In each case, they believed the Bible is true and that God would heal them. Each was surrounded by people praying for their healing and each knew of many other cases when God had healed serious diseases. Yet, with these specific people, they died. They died believing for healing. Why did they die before old age?

This time it was me posing the question to God. "Why did these people die? They believed your Word. Your Word says Jesus bore stripes for our healing. If your Word is true and they believed it, why did they die?"

Oh, the glory of our God! He loves us so much! If we will only listen, there is so much He wants to reveal! Do you remember when Jesus said to His disciples, "I have so much more to tell you, but you are not ready?"[2] Prepare yourself so He can tell you more and more!

He was kind enough to answer my probing question.

Believing, or Believing

Most people who are believing God for something like physical healing of the body have a passive sense of believing. They are sitting back, trusting God to take care of the situation. I have heard people say, "God's got this!" or "God will take care of it!" They know He has the power to heal and deep inside they trust that God will choose to heal them. Sounds like they are believing God, doesn't it?

The problem is that is a natural human form of believing. It's a=b, b=c, so a=c all over again. This thinking proceeds from logical head knowledge, and there is no supernatural power in human logic.

There is another kind of believing, the kind that God is relying on us to have. This believing is an active form of believing, full of supernatural power. It transpires when your "believing" goes past your brain and gets down deep in your spirit.

Active believers resist the Devil with God's Word at every turn. They take up the Word of God which is the sword of the Spirit and wield it to stop Satan's attacks. They have a deep abiding trust resulting from abiding in Him and know in their gut (not their head) that God's Word will stop the schemes of the devil. Active believers do not sit back and wait on God to do something. They know He already did something, sending His Son to conquer the enemy and make a triumph over him. Jesus took those stripes for healing and carried illness and bore pains when he hung on that tree. It is finished. The victory is won. Knowing God has done His part, active believers do their part, taking up that sword as warriors on the battlefield of life.

Active believers resist the devil in their bodies and in their minds using the Word of God.

Supernatural believers stand on the truth of God's Word for every aspect of life, relying on the immeasurable greatness of God's power made available to us who believe,[3] knowing God can do far more abundantly than we can ask or think according to His power at work within us.[4] His power is made available, but we must take that power and work it. He promises He watches over his Word to perform it.[5] You wield His Word like a sword at the enemy, and He watches over it to perform it. You speak it out in faith, He does what He says in that spoken Word to overcome the enemy's attack.

To walk in that power, you must believe God's Word. If you only believe with your head, you will not be able to use the Word as a weapon against the enemy. Doubt and anxiety will arise with human believing. Nothing human has power over the enemy. Only God - His authority and Word - has power over the enemy.

Perhaps you realize like I did that you have a little problem with your "believer." Do not be discouraged. To the contrary, it's time to get excited! Once you realize that you have not been truly believing like you thought you were, you have opened yourself to opportunities for God to reveal more of His truth to you. He wants you to move from passive believing to active believing, and He will lead you there. Let Him challenge you with scriptures that test your "believer." Once you break through your brain barrier and begin believing in your spirit, God's power will manifest more in your life.

Remember when Peter and John encountered the lame man at the temple gate?

> But Peter said, "I have no silver and gold,
> but what I do have I give to you.
> In the name of Jesus Christ of Nazareth,
> rise up and walk!"
>
> Acts 3:6

Peter not only spoke, but he knew what he had. He believed what Jesus had taught him about speaking to the mountain. It was not a knowledge in his head, it was a knowing in his spirit.

Biggest Hinderance to Power

What you experience in this natural world and what the Word of God says will usually conflict. You face the same question Elisha faced when the Syrian army surrounded his city (chapter four).[6] Which will you believe? Will you follow your natural inclinations and believe what you see with your natural eyes? Yes, the entire Syrian army came to get two lonely men.

Yes, the situation in the natural is dire, impossible to survive. In the natural, Elisha and his servant would be dead before sundown.

Elisha believed God over what his natural eyes told him. Will you dare to believe God's Word like Elisha did? Because he chose to believe God, looking beyond the natural, he singlehandedly took the entire Syrian army to his king as prisoners of war. That is power! That is the truth of the supernatural realm. God's supreme power reigns. And He made that power available to you, if you can get past human head-level passive believing and step into supernatural active believing. Want to know the secret to getting there?

Look back at first scripture quoted in this chapter. It is as follows:

> *Therefore I tell you,*
> *whatever you ask in prayer,*
> *believe that you have received it,*
> *and it will be yours.*
>
> Mark 11:24

Did I read that correctly? Jesus said I must *believe* I will receive it, *then – only then* – I will receive it. That sounds backwards to me. In human terms it is backwards. In supernatural terms, it is what is required to receive that for which you pray. Believe it first. Receive it if you can believe for it.

Jesus teaches us we cannot just quote scriptures and expect the supernatural to penetrate the veil. We cannot just say we believe the Word. We must also not doubt. We must not rely on the natural circumstances we see with our natural eyes. We must believe God's Word. If you do not doubt, you will believe it is done. In the supernatural it is already done. All you must do is believe it in your spirit (this is the place where you believe it without anxiety and worry over what you see with your natural eyes) and you will receive it. Your faith becomes the only eyes you rely on.

> *You have to believe God's Word*
> *until the believing gets past your head*
> *and down into your spirit*

This process is a part of the renewal of your mind. You spend so much time in the Word until you begin to think like Jesus thinks, act like Jesus acts, and believe like Jesus believes. You will have the mind of Christ.[7] When you pray, you will receive that which you pray for. Satan's schemes will fail in your life, and his attacks will be thwarted from your family.

Are you beginning to see how powerful God's Word truly is? I see a hunger for Jesus Christ building up in you. The more secrets you learn, the easier it will be to prioritize time with God in your busy schedule. After a while, you wonder how you ever lived without spending time with Him.

While this vision of your new life in Christ Jesus forms in your mind and your spirit, we must look at another vital key for victory in the Kingdom of God. In chapter four, you discovered the source of God's power is contained in the Kingdom of God. In this next secret, you will learn the strength of that Kingdom. This secret is the engine for the power of God. Without it, you will stumble under the greatness of the power. With it, the immeasurable greatness of His power will be at your disposal and you will be ready to experience it.

ENDNOTES

[1]Matthew 19:16 And behold, a man came up to him, saying, "Teacher, what good deed must I do to have eternal life?" Mark 10:17 And as he was setting out on his journey, a man ran up and knelt before him and asked him, "Good Teacher, what must I do to inherit eternal life?"

[2]John 16:12 "I still have many things to say to you, but you cannot bear them now.

[3]Ephesians 1:18-19 having the eyes of your hearts enlightened, that you may know what is the hope to which he has called you, what are the riches of his glorious inheritance in the saints, and what is the immeasurable greatness of his power toward us who believe, according to the working of his great might.

[4]Ephesians 3:20 Now to him who is able to do far more abundantly than all that we ask or think, according to the power at work within us,

[5]Jeremiah 1:12 Then the LORD said to me, "You have seen well, for I am watching over my word to perform it."

[6]2 Kings 6:15-17 When the servant of the man of God rose early in the morning and went out, behold, an army with horses and chariots was all around the city. And the servant said, "Alas, my master! What shall we do?" He said, "Do not be afraid, for those who are with us are more than those who are with them." Then Elisha prayed and said, "O LORD, please open his eyes that he may see." So the LORD opened the eyes of the young man, and he saw, and behold, the mountain was full of horses and chariots of fire all around Elisha.

[7]1 Corinthians 2:16 "For who has understood the mind of the Lord so as to instruct him?" But we have the mind of Christ.

Chapter 10

Secret Number Seven

Authority

You have learned six secrets to God's power and how to experience it in your life. You understand the power is contained in God's Kingdom and you have new spiritual eyes whereby you see that Kingdom. You no longer rely on human power, because you are acutely aware it is Jesus Who does all the work of the Kingdom through your hands, mouth and feet. Time in God's presence has become a top priority in your household and your schedule reflects changes you are making so you can spend time with Him.

Nestled within the secrets were three power stations where you have started to build spiritual muscles. You feed on the Word of God and see it as the substance of life. Jesus is the Word made manifest; therefore, the Word is alive, and the Word renews your mind into the likeness of Jesus. You are training with your newly appointed weapon, the Sword of the Spirit, which is the Word of God.

I expect you are gaining more understanding about how God's Kingdom works and feel stronger in your Christian walk. Now you are beginning to see why your prayers were not previously answered, and why God's promises seemed evasive, if not completely unobtainable. Fresh hope fills you as the reality of God's promises are in view.

Enjoy the excitement, because we still have one more secret to reveal!

The Sword

God placed a weapon in your hand. It was not an easy task to get this weapon to you, for Jesus had to suffer severely to get it to you. Your sword, the Word of God, is not to be placed on a shelf while you go about the world's business. It is not meant to decorate your bookcase while you are stomped down by the enemy, giving in to Satan's ways, thoughts and deeds. Jesus suffered to get you this weapon and He fully expects you to pick it up, like a knight in the heat of battle, and use it to protect the portion of the Kingdom assigned to you – your life, your family, your sphere of influence in this world.

There is a secret to the power in that sword. By looking at the Kingdom we can discover the secret of the power.

Three Major Mindsets

Let me begin by showing you the three major mindsets I have discovered in our society in modern times. The first I call a government mindset. With this mindset, people are looking to the government to take care of them and meet their needs. I am not adverse to the government assisting people who need help, nor am I suggesting people who need assistance should not accept the government's help. By all means, the system is there for a purpose. It does pose a problem for Christians that can unsuspectingly hinder their walk. While getting help from the government, you can easily fall into the trap of depending on the government. A mindset develops where you look to the government for your well-being, provision and care. You are not looking to God as your ultimate provider. God and God alone should be the one you turn your heart to when you are in need.

The second mindset I discovered may be the most predominate. I refer to it as the American mindset. This is the "me" mindset where ultimate success is defined by what I can accomplish. I am my own boss. I can do it. I did it myself. I am in control of my life. I decide what I will or will not do. No one tells me what to do and certainly no one is going to control my life. Our society promotes this mindset, from Hollywood to Washington, D.C. to the fields of pro sports. It is practically worshipped in America, and those who appear successful are placed on thrones to be adored by the masses. Ultimate success in this country is often defined by the ability to avoid all responsibility to another person. With the American mindset one depends on self for needs, provision, protection and solutions. God is shoved to the back burner, only to be pulled out when all else fails. Rather than depending on God, He becomes a resource of last resort.

Both mindsets described here depower our Christian lives, because they are totally contrary to the Word of God. To walk in God's power, you must have God's mindset and operate according to God's Word. The best the government or self can manage to do for you pales in comparison to the power of God in your life.

God reveals the mindset He wants for you in the establishment of His Kingdom. In a Kingdom mindset, there is an ultimate authority called a King and all else are His subjects. As a subject to King Jesus, you live for one purpose – to fulfill the will of your King. Your only priority is to accomplish what He assigns you or places in your care. As subjects of the King, you clear your lives of anything except what the King desires, needs or assigns. Because of His great love for you, every assignment is for your best interest. Everything He leads you to do, every response, every act benefits you and your family if you will only trust Him and obey.

In the garden of Eden, it is Satan who sowed the seeds of selfishness, suggesting we could be like God. Satan is the one who places pride of what self can accomplish over the will and desires of God.

God placed in you specific talents and abilities, but they are not for your own gratification and glory, they are to equip you to accomplish the destiny He ordained for your life from the foundation of the world. With a Kingdom mindset you take your talents and focus on God's opinion, His work, His glory and His Word.

In exchange, you have the power of the King, the protection of his army, and provision made available from the riches of His treasures. (If you are right now imagining big mansions and fast cars, the American mindset is at work in you.) God's glory radiates through your family, providing peace in your heart and stability of your mind.

Secret Number Seven

Secret to the power of the Sword - It is all based on God's Authority

Within this Kingdom is the secret to the power of your God-issued sword.

> *And he called to him his twelve disciples*
> *and gave them authority*
> *over unclean spirits, to cast them out,*
> *and to heal every disease and every affliction.*
>
> *Matthew 10:1*

Jesus sends His subjects out into the world to accomplish His work. What is the first thing He does? He gives them His authority. Then he sends them out with a task list.

> *And proclaim as you go, saying,*
> *'The kingdom of heaven is at hand.'*
> *Heal the sick,*
> *raise the dead,*
> *cleanse lepers,*
> *cast out demons...*
>
> *Matthew 10:7-8*

That is quite an interesting job description! Who were these guys to get a job like that done? They were fishermen, not Pharisees. They were primarily uneducated in the Scriptures. What did Jesus do to prepare them? Certainly, He had been training them for some time. Yet, at the moment He was releasing them to go, the primary thing He handed them was His authority.

Think about a Kingdom. A king has a proposition to offer another king. The king then appoints his messenger to act as ambassador to deliver the message. That ambassador has the authority of the king on him for that mission. He goes to the foreign land and speaks for the king, signs for the king, and enforces the king's words. This messenger has no power in and of himself. He is not worthy to stand in a king's presence. Yet he goes before the foreign king with confidence because he has something given him. All his power to stand before, make contracts with, and negotiate with foreign leaders is derived from the authority his king has placed on him.

Consider these scriptures in light of our current discussion.

In my name they will cast out demons

Mark 16:17

****

Whatever you ask in my name, this I will do, that the Father may be glorified in the Son.

John 14:13

****

> *If you ask me anything in my name,*
> *I will do it.*
>
> John 14:14

****

> *I chose you and appointed you*
> *that you should go and bear fruit*
> *and that your fruit should abide,*
> *so that whatever you ask the Father in my name,*
> *he may give it to you.*
>
> John 15:16

****

> *Truly, truly, I say to you,*
> *whatever you ask of the Father in my name,*
> *he will give it to you.*
>
> John 16:23

Are you picking up on the emphasis here? The key words Jesus speaks is, "In My Name." Jesus tells you that you can do anything He assigns you if you do it under the authority of His name.

This reminds me of police officers patrolling our cities and highways. Some of our finest citizens are these men and women who risk their lives to protect us. They are regular people just like you and me. If you saw them off duty, you would not think anything special about them. You may not notice them at all. If one of them yelled at you commanding you to do something, you would probably laugh it off. There would be no reason to listen to what they tell you to do.

Let them don their uniform and secure their badge and the whole picture changes. Now when they yell for you to stop, you listen and obey quickly. What changed? Why would you blow them off at one time and quickly respond at another point in time?

Authority.

These officers have the authority of the state behind them. With this authority they can arrest you, ticket you, or detain you. Their words have authority to stop you in your tracks.

"Stop in the name of the law!"

When you hear those words, you will stop or pay the consequences. You do not stop because of who they are, but because of the authority given to them by a higher power. It is because of the power of the state that what they say comes to pass.

"Be healed in the name of Jesus!"

"Be cast out in the name of Jesus!"

You heard those kinds of words before and might have even questioned their validity, but this is the purpose of why they are spoken in this way. I am a nobody in the universe, but I have been bestowed by God with His authority to speak in His name for specific tasks according to His will. Since every knee bows at the name of Jesus, and all are subjected under His feet, demons must obey when He speaks. It is no matter if He speaks His authority through your mouth. The authority is still just as powerful. We are Jesus body now: His hands, His feet and His mouth. When we speak in His name, anything subjected to His name must obey.

This is the confidence we have to believe what we speak as coming to pass. Remember this passage in Acts.

> *I have no silver and gold,*
> *but what I do have I give to you.*
> *In the name of Jesus Christ of Nazareth,*
> *rise up and walk!"*

Acts 3:6

Peter said, "What I do have I give to you." What Peter had was the authority of Jesus Christ. He invoked that authority by commanding the man to rise up and walk in the name of Jesus Christ. I dare say, that was tremendously more valuable for that lame man than any amount of silver or gold.

It is vitally important you realize these are not magic words place at your disposal to use as you please. The king's ambassador has limits to what he can say or do. He may not step outside the boundaries of what his king has authorized him to accomplish, or he could lose his head. In the same way, if you step outside the boundaries of what God's authority dictates, you will find yourself powerless, vulnerable and rebellious. It is illegal for a police officer to misrepresent his power or use it outside the boundaries of the state's intended use of it. If he does, he can find himself suffering the consequences of abuse of power. In the same way, you must be careful to keep your heart and intentions focused on God's intended use of this authority to overcome the enemy in your life and set captives free.

Authority is the secret to the power of your sword. You speak out God's Word with faith, not doubting because of your confidence in the authority of Jesus Christ. And what you say comes to pass. With this fully-powered sword, you face enemy attacks with confidence and stop his schemes cold.

With a Kingdom mindset, you let go of dependence on anything or anyone but your almighty God. No earthly riches compare to your walk as a powerful Christian. You seek first the Kingdom of God, its King, power and authority, and all these things are added unto you.[1]

Time to Step Out in Power

Congratulations! You are now a vessel made ready to experience the power of God flowing through your life! In order to move forward, you must look back and continue working with the power stations. Build those spiritual muscles until they bulk up to handle more and more of God's power. The more you prepare, the more power God will place in your hands. He will not give you more than you are ready for. But with continued workouts, you will see more and more power flow through you and feel the exhilaration of the victorious life in Christ Jesus!

The next two chapters will show you how to get that power pump primed in your life and get the flow going. When the pump turns on, changes begin to happen in the circumstances of your life. All you need to do is trust God at His Word and choose His way over the world's way. Choose life over death.

Choose the supernatural over the natural. Don't give up. Keep pressing deeper into God's Kingdom and His Word.

Are you ready to begin walking in God's power? Then read on because the moment of stepping into the power has finally arrived.

ENDNOTES

[1] Matthew 6:33 But seek first the kingdom of God and his righteousness, and all these things will be added to you.

Chapter 11

Powerful Christians Pray It Out

Your spiritual eyes are opening to the majesty and glory of God's amazing creation, both natural and supernatural. You see behind the veil of perception and understand what supernatural really refers to.

You have learned a lot and may have already noticed changes in how you speak, pray or respond to others, simply because you have experienced a paradigm shift and can now "see" or understand beyond the veil of perception in what we call the supernatural. You have taken first steps in working with the secret power stations. Like any power building program, you must continue exercising with the power stations to build more and more strength in each of the areas discussed.

Hunger for God's Word grows inside you because you understand its importance at a deeper level. You desire to get into it and stay in it because the Word is Jesus Christ and you must abide in Him for life. You want your mind renewed in the Word, so you can be transformed into the likeness of your Savior. The Word is alive, dividing soul and spirit so you are able to hear God's voice clearly.

You see your weapon, the sword of the Spirit. You feel it in your hands and understand the source of its power. As you fill your arsenal with more of the Word, you speak it out, using that sword more skillfully with each use, rousting demons, healing the sick and protecting your family.

You are testing what you believe about the Bible, allowing God to challenge you about scripture portions. You want your Bible knowledge to go past your head and get deep into your spirit so that you are an active believer and not a passive believer. When the natural world conflicts with what the Word of God says, you believe the Word no matter what your natural eyes see. You are relying more on faith as your sight and less on your eyeballs. Your eyes of faith are becoming stronger every day.

Finally, you understand the supreme authority that you have voluntarily place yourself under. You know that when you speak the Word, the immeasurable greatness of God's power backs up His every word as you speak it out boldly with confidence. You perceive the dangers of stepping outside the boundaries of that authority by misrepresenting it or using it for your own gain.

This is the moment you have been waiting for. It is time to start the power pump flowing in your life. Take all that you have learned in this book and begin by applying it to your prayers.

Speak it Out

When I was young, the only person I ever heard pray out loud was the priest of our hometown Episcopal church. Those prayers were rather ritualistic, only spoken at predesignated times during a service, and quite often quoted from a prayer book rather than from the heart. The only other prayers I heard spoken out loud were around the dinner table at night in our home, where we children repeated the same exact ditty. "God is good. God is great. Let us thank Him for our food. Amen." Once my brother and I were old enough to have the hang of it ourselves, our parents were silent during this repetitious routine for the remaining years of our childhood.

The thought of speaking out loud to pray was foreign to me. Quite often at our old hometown church, we would have a moment of corporate prayer. This was a time when the entire church fell deafly silent as everyone bowed their head to pray in their minds. No one spoke a word. You could hear the slightest foot shuffle on those old wooden floors of our grand historic cathedral. Though it felt like an hour, never did it last more than thirty to sixty seconds.

Half way through elementary school, my parents found a clever way to put us in a private school we had no money for. My mother went to work for the school. With the employee discount applied, her entire paycheck managed to cover the tuition. I found myself thrust into the halls and walls of a Baptist parochial school. Things were different there, as I heard for the first time someone pray out loud an unscripted prayer.

After I grew up, I visited a charismatic sort of church with friends. There I heard fiery sorts of prayers all prayed out loud with lots of gusto and feeling expressed. This was shocking and awkward for me with my background. Not me! Not in a million years!

Over time I softened and eventually stuck my toe in the pool of audible praying. Once I did it a little bit, the awkwardness slowly melted away, and eventually I had no problem praying out loud. When I married, I was able to pray with my new husband. We both acted a little embarrassed at first, but within a short time were in full swing of daily prayer life together.

When I first learned about hagah[1] - speaking out the Word of God constantly - I felt that same old uncomfortable feeling all over again. By then I had children in the house and I was not going to look like a crazy lady to them! What might they say to their Grandma?

I was faced with one of those life vs death / natural vs supernatural choices. If speaking out the Word of God was the only way to become a powerful Christian, then I resolved that nothing else mattered to me. I was more concerned about what God thought of me than what my children or even my mother-in-law thought of me. Joshua 1:8 told me it would make my way prosperous and I will have good success if I hagah the Word day and night. My children would get used to it. They did, much quicker than I expected. Now they have the strength of hagah modeled for them daily and are beginning to pick up on it for themselves.

You might be faced with one of those choices right now. If the thought of praying out loud seems difficult and distressing, think of the reality of the choice set before you. Can you push through some discomfort to achieve greater things in Christ Jesus? I dare say most of our Christian walk involves many such moments. The reality of the dangers outside our realm of perception is reason enough to suck it up, for ourselves and for our households. The promises of God's goodness and favor are more than enough enticement to push through whatever God requires us to bring us to completion.

Pray According to the Word

When you hagah the Word of God day and night, two things are happening. First, you are praying. To speak God's Word constantly is to abide in Jesus Christ. There is much communication happening between God's Spirit and your spirit when you do this. The Holy Spirit is building you up, revealing meaning of scriptures to you, and training you in the use of those scriptures for when you find yourself on the battlefield. Since praying is communicating with God and it is obvious that when you hagah the Word communication happens, then hagah is a form of praying.

I might be busy at a sink full of dishes, speaking out the Word, I am praying.[2] I can be driving to the grocery store, walking my neighborhood, or folding clothes. If I hagah the Word while I do those things, I am enjoying a vigorous and healthy prayer life.

Second, this practice of hagah prepares me for engagement with the enemy. The Holy Spirit trains me in that Word. He leads me to scriptures to fill my arsenal, brings them up to my remembrance, and engages my imagination to show me how it might be used against the enemy. This is my boot camp experience. I am running through the moves, but not with a real enemy. Later, when I do encounter the enemy, I am prepared. Those words just roll off my tongue with ease and destroy demonic forces.

Here is an extreme example, but an example nonetheless. I have seen tremendous miracles God has done by my hand so far, but I have not yet seen a person set free from a wheelchair. I know God has predestined me to be used in this way, because He has the Holy Spirit preparing me. I have scriptures building up in my arsenal, and in my imagination I see myself using those scriptures as I pray over people in wheelchairs. In my imagination they rise up, set free from that bondage. When the moment truly comes that I have opportunity to pray for someone in a wheelchair, I will be a soldier prepared for that battle, will engage the enemy, and Jesus will set that captive free from their natural bondage. It all starts with my willingness to hagah the Word, communicating with God day and night.

It is not just sickness He prepares you for. Many times, the Holy Spirit prepares us for encountering an irritable or mean person, a character issue with our children, or a distressing situation with our spouse. Hagah the Word and give the Holy Spirit freedom and permission to prepare your heart and mind for what He knows you will face. When the battle goes live, your response will be a Godly one that sets all the wheels in motion on your behalf beyond that supernatural veil.

The most important thing about praying in power is that you pray according to His will. The first time I prayed for someone to have a deaf ear opened, I did not have this preparation time with the Holy Spirit. I simply prayed with boldness according to God's Word. A lady approached me at a meeting for prayer for her ear. This was totally new to me and I had no confidence in myself to pray for her. But this I did know - God did not intend for this ear to be deaf. I knew deep in my spirit it was the enemy who seeks to steal, kill and destroy. With confidence in God's will, I prayed against the enemy with the arsenal I had. I spoke to her mountain like Peter spoke to the lame man.[3] The lady and I heard a sound like a pop, and she beamed with excitement as she proclaimed she could now hear out of that ear.

Be careful what words you choose to use when praying. To be a powerful Christian is to use Gods power by using God's words and pray according to how Jesus taught us to pray when he revealed the secret of speaking to the mountain.[4]

Most people who pray for sickness pray something along these lines. "Dear God, please heal Mrs. Smith. She loves you and she serves in this church all the time. She is so good with the children. They all love her so much. We know you love her, so we are asking you to reach down from heaven and touch her for healing. Please keep her comfortable so she doesn't suffer. Thank you for Mrs. Smith. Please heal her. In Jesus name. Amen."

What a sweet-sounding prayer! The problem is "sweet" is not where the power is. Without God's power, it is not effective. Christians know it too, because they call everyone they know and ask them to pray for Mrs. Smith to be healed. I guess they figure if enough people coerce God, He will bend under the pressure and be forced to concede and heal Mrs. Smith.

God is not sitting in heaven deciding who He might decide to pick for healing, and who He will overlook. He is not obstinately refusing to heal Mrs. Smith. He is not vulnerable to manipulation from people, no matter how many chide in with their arm-twisting excuses for why He should pick Mrs. Smith to be healed. He is not favoring one man's prayers over another, and He is certainly not waiting for some magic number of people to rally around poor Mrs. Smith so that He will finally relent and heal her. That is an unbiblical picture derived from ignorance of the supernatural reality beyond the veil.

When you hagah daily, the Holy Spirit builds you up so that when you pray for the sick, He is directing your prayer. No one better than the Holy Spirit to choose the words for a prayer for a healing, don't you agree?

A powerful Christian might pray a prayer something like this. "God you are a majestic and holy God.[5] There is no one like you, none as powerful[6] or as loving[7] or as merciful[8] as you. We know you love Mrs. Smith[9] and have already paid the price[10] to set her free from this attack. We thank you Jesus for taking those stripes for her healing.[11] So in the name of Jesus, by the power and authority of Jesus Christ (now looking at Mrs. Smith and laying hands on her) I speak to this sickness and command you to leave her body. I command cancer to die in the powerful name of Jesus. Jesus already carried her sickness and bore her pain.[12] So you must leave her body now. No weapon formed against Mrs. Smith will prosper, but this voice that rises up to judge her, we condemn in Jesus name.[13] Thank you, God, for your power and mercy for this precious saint. Thank you for sending Jesus to take every part of the curse and nail it to that tree.[14] Mrs. Smith, by the power of God in the name of Jesus, stand up and be healed."[15]

That is not a magic potion, nor is it something to memorize and use repeatedly. It is an off-the-cuff made up example of how a powerful prayer might sound. A powerful prayer is led by the Holy Spirit, Who pulls from the arsenal *you* have assembled through abiding in Jesus Christ, the Word. You speak it with authority, believing every portion of quoted scripture is more real than the pitiful condition of Mrs. Smith's body in front of you. This is an example of wielding your sword at the enemy and stopping his attack.

Another word of caution about praying according to God's Word. The Holy Spirit never leads you to pray with bitterness, resentment or hate, because He does not see the ornery obnoxious person as the problem. He sees the spirit influencing that person as the real enemy according to Ephesians.[16] Be careful that your prayers don't sound something like this: "Dear God, did you see what that rascal did to me? I pray that you set him straight for me. Make sure he cannot do that to me or anyone else again. Give him what he deserves, God. I thank you for helping me. Amen." Remember the words of Jesus when he told us to love our enemies, do good to those who mistreat you and bless those who curse you. He meant what He said, because the real enemy is not the human rascal, but the spirit of the air that you cannot see influencing the human to act in that particular way. When you love, do good, and bless, you are effectively landing unseen blows on an invisible enemy. This is really what Jesus is commanding you to do. Sock it to the enemy.

What About Sickness?

I think it appropriate to address a prevalent issue in the body of Christ of which there is much confusion. That is the question of God's will in sickness. So many Christians believe they should humble themselves and accept sickness as a way God is trying to teach them something. I absolutely, adamantly wholeheartedly do not agree.

Sickness was not a part of the original creation in the Garden. Sickness is a part of the process of death, so sickness was not introduced into the world until sin was introduced, bringing with it death. Anything rooted in Satan's deception is not a tool God uses to teach us.

Satan is the father of sickness, death, lies and destruction. It is Satan who seeks to steal, kill and destroy. Satan lurks around seeing who he may devour.

We do see God telling us such things can come to pass, such as in the blessings and curses introduced in Deuteronomy 28. This is not because God dishes out sickness. It is because if you are not living according to His ways, you are outside of the divine protection of his shelter. It leaves you vulnerable to the enemy. It is like the chick who runs out from beneath the shelter of the mother hen's wing. The chick is now on his own, by his own choice, and is vulnerable to the hawk. To choose to not follow God's Word is to choose not to accept His walkie talkie. Sickness is a big landmine out there, one of Satan's craftiest tricks.

It is true that anything Satan intends for our destruction, God can use for His glory.[17] I do believe when Satan attacks our body with sickness or disease, God's power working through His people brings a testimony that, according to Revelation,[18] conquers the enemy. God's glory is revealed, people come to know Him, and Satan is defeated. This is what often causes confusion when Christians think God is making them sick to teach them something. It is true we do learn something. The trial does mature us and complete us so that we are not lacking anything.[19] But it is an incorrect assumption that, because good came out of the situation, it means God did it. Every good and perfect gift comes from God.[20] Sickness is neither good nor perfect.

If it were true that God made you sick, then wouldn't it be a sin to pray that it be taken away? If God wants you sick, you should walk it out, accept it, and never pray for your healing because it would be praying against His will. Everything we pray must be according to His will. Why then, would Jesus command those who believe to lay hands on the sick for them to recover? Would Jesus teach to work against the will of the Father? To the contrary, Jesus said He did nothing unless He heard it from the Father.

On the other hand, if it is Satan who brings this attack against us, then God is well pleased with the servant who stands up against this foe, wielding God's hand-fashioned weapon using it to destroy that scheme against a human life. Laying hands on the sick for their recovery would be in obedience to the Son to the glory of the Father by the power of the Holy Spirit.

If sickness comes on your body, you can choose to go to the doctors and I am in no way suggesting that you don't. I am telling you that there is another way to battle sickness that is more effective than the doctors' methods. Until you are practiced at walking in God's power, I recommend that you do seek doctors. We are not called to be foolish. Only you know if you have been practicing this walk of faith and are ready to believe for your healing. If you are going to doctors, just be sure to pay close attention to the words you speak over yourself. I personally would never say, "I have cancer" but I might say, "the doctor says I have cancer, but in Jesus name it has no power over me." Then I would command it to die.

I want to share one last word about sickness. I expressed how animate I am that sickness came in the garden with the fall of man because sickness is a part of the cycle of death, and death was brought by sin. No matter what the doctors say about the physical nature of the sickness, no matter what pictures they show, or laboratory reports they produce, I know sickness at its very root comes from sin. So, if I had to categorize it as either good or evil, it obviously falls under evil. Knowing sickness is rooted in evil, and knowing evil wants to kill, steal and destroy, I know sickness is always rooted in an evil (or unclean) spirit. I have no reason to worry about praying against God's will, for I know God earnestly desires for people to walk in health. The church swells with power the day it wakes up and fights the true enemy. Imagine the body of Christ without sickness. How much could the church accomplish in this world if every member were strong and healthy? How much of the church's resources of time and energy would be rerouted to real Kingdom work if it were not being spent so heavily on Christian sickness? I can only imagine.

Thankfulness

My final thought on praying according to the Word is to remember to always pray with thanksgiving. This is so important that Paul repeats it in multiple letters.

...do not be anxious about anything,
but in everything by prayer and supplication
with thanksgiving
let your requests be made known to God.

Philippians 4:6

****

Continue steadfastly in prayer,
being watchful in it with thanksgiving.

Colossians 4:2

****

First of all, then, I urge that
supplications,
prayers,
intercessions,

> *and thanksgivings*
> *be made for all people,*
>
> *1 Timothy 2:1*

Paul urges believers to always approach God with thanksgiving. It is with thanksgiving that we are able to enter God's gates.[21] Thankfulness keeps you in a place of humbleness and prevents pride from puffing you up, so you are made ready to come before Him.

> *But this is the one to whom I will look:*
> *he who is humble*
> *and contrite in spirit*
> *and trembles at my word.*
>
> *Isaiah 66:2*

Types of Prayers

We have already addressed some of these, but I find it fitting to recap different types and forms of prayers. Remember, praying to God is simply communication with God. Just like communication between humans, there are many forms of communication that can take place.

Setting aside quiet time to talk with God

When you hear the word "prayer," this is what most people envision. Taking time to sit and talk with God gives you great opportunity to bring your supplications to God and chat with Him about your needs.[22] There are many ways to go about this.

One is to model your prayer after the Lord's prayer where He taught His disciples a form of prayer.[23] Take each of the verses, quote it, and then fill in how it applies to your life. For example, when you reach the verse that mentions being protected from temptation, name your temptations. Ask Him for help with that specific thing you struggle with. Make it personal between you and Him.

The model I use most is based on Psalm 100,[24] enter His gates with thanksgiving and enter His courts with praise. I open my prayer time with thanksgiving for specific things He has done for me. This could be something spectacular He just did on my behalf, or as simple as the breath in my lungs today. Let thanksgiving pour out to Him. Then enter His courts with praise. Now my attention turns to praising Him for Who He is. This has nothing to do with me and everything to do with Him. I often imagine the gates and court of the tabernacle or temple as I pray this way. After I have entered His courts, then I make my requests known[25] and talk them out with Him.

There doesn't have to be a model at all. Just talk with God. He longs for fellowship with you. If you will meet with Him, He will gladly join you there, no matter how it looks.

Remember, prayer is communication, and communication is a two-way conversation. There must be time to sit and listen. Sometimes, I put on worship music, enter His gates with Thanksgiving and His courts with praise, then sit quietly and listen. I listen for scripture meanings He wants to reveal, jobs He wants me to accomplish, or the love He wants to pour over me.

Prayer for needs and provision

This may look like the type of prayer described above, but there is a more intensity to the requests, because of a dire need for provision or an answer or solution to a problem. Remember, pray believing the promises in scripture for what He has already done. No need to ask for Him to do something He has already done for you. If you ask for what He has already done, it is like admitting that you do not really believe that part of the Bible. If Jesus took stripes for your healing, God already came down and carried that sickness to the cross. To ask for Him to do anything more is to say what He did is not good enough. Never counter what the Bible says.

If you are praying about a need the Bible has already addressed, pray in faith. If you need a job, food or other provision, pray according to the Word, "I have never seen God's righteous forsaken or His children begging for bread[26] so I thank you God for providing for my family. Thank you that you bless my basket and my kneading bowl.[27] I thank you that you have lined up that provision. I know you have everything I need for my family." Many a family has seen the miracle of provision believing God at His Word in such ways.

Praying for healing and other enemy attacks

We have discussed these types of prayers in much detail, because this is where we see powerful Christians on the battlefield. Ephesians 6 addresses this battle directly. I recommend you spend some time abiding in that portion of scripture. We concentrated on the true enemy mentioned in verses 11 and 12, and the sword of the Spirit in verse 17, yet there are plenty more riches yet to be gleaned from Ephesians 6.

I wrote a book entitled *My Favorite Weapons* with some of my favorite scripture portions for the battlefield. You can get it for free just for reading this book.[28]

I am a servant of Most High God and as such, I am the one waiting to hear His voice and respond to the call. Many Christians have this reversed. Their prayer life sounds like they are invoking a butler to do their bidding. God is not a divine butler waiting in the wings to jump to your service; however, God does watch over His word to perform it.[29] Ministering angels are at His command and, just like Elisha facing the Syrian army, God's host stands ready to serve their Master as He orders them into service on the behalf of powerful Christians that believe their God, wield their sword, and stand under authority.

One Final Disclaimer - Mansions and Mercedes

Satan corrupts God's truth as one of his major landmines. Be careful lest you fall into his trap. In the area of believing, we must remember the reason for our prayers and why God has made His immeasurable power available to us. The Kingdom has work to be accomplished and you have been designated from the foundation of the world to fulfill your destiny in His Kingdom. In the Kingdom, God does provide for all we need, including provision, protection and rescue.

If you ask and do not receive, you must consider your heart and the motivation behind your prayers.

*You ask and do not receive,
because you ask wrongly,*

to spend it on your passions.

James 4:3

God is not an ATM machine for you to pull out riches for your own pleasures. If you pray to receive to fulfill your own passions, be careful, as God's power does not exist in anything human. God's power is for Kingdom purposes. If you pray for needs or to accomplish His Kingdom work, the power will flow in your life. If you expect fast cars, a exquisite home, or retaliation against an adversary, the power flow shuts down.

Glamour and riches are greatly overrated. This phenomenon is due to the American mindset I described in chapter 10. God is not so impressed with ritzy glamour. Nor does He see the need for it in the Kingdom. If your eyes are set on Jesus Christ your only hope, you will not be focused on worldly treasures either.

Not that I am speaking of being in need,
for I have learned in whatever situation I am
to be content.
I know how to be brought low,
and I know how to abound.
In any and every circumstance,
I have learned the secret of facing plenty and hunger,
abundance and need.

Philippians 4:11-12

****

But godliness with contentment is great gain,

1 Timothy 6:6

****

*But if we have food and clothing,
with these we will be content.*

1 Timothy 6:8

Paul indicates there were times he lived in plenty. But His focus was not on those things. He was able to walk among the riches and not be swayed or tempted because all that mattered to him was Jesus Christ and Him crucified.[30] Paul was just as content with riches as he was when he was in need. Paul had a keen awareness that nothing the world has to offer compares to the promises in God. How much money would it take for you to give up that walkie talkie? How much money would you take in exchange for the host of heaven to be working on your behalf? For me, no amount of money in the world is worth the surpassing riches we have in Jesus Christ.

Stick With It

It may take time and patience as you learn to adjust your prayer language. Do not give up. The payoff is incredible as you learn to function powerfully in God's Kingdom, mounding up crowns to lay at Jesus feet, awaiting those sweet words, "Well done good and faithful servant. Enter into the joy of your King!"

To assure that you experience hearing those amazing words on the appointed day, I must show you the most powerful aspect of all God's Kingdom. There is nothing that can withstand what I am about to show you, and Satan is very aware of the danger he faces when you learn it and live it, because with it you are unstoppable. His greatest onslaught against God comes by attacking humans through this avenue.

God depends on you to take all you have learned and begin to utilize His power for the Kingdom, but if it is not done according to what you learn in the next chapter, you will have gained absolutely nothing. To God, nothing is of more paramount importance in all the universe.

ENDNOTES

[1] Chapter 8 subheading "David Spoke the Word

[2] KingdomPurposeLife.com/cud – Enjoy reading the entire lighthearted yet enlightening article.

[3] Chapters 8 and 10, Acts 3:6 But Peter said, "I have no silver and gold, but what I do have I give to you. In the name of Jesus Christ of Nazareth, rise up and walk!"

[4] Chapter 8, Mark 11:23 Truly, I say to you, whoever says to this mountain, 'Be taken up and thrown into the sea,' and does not doubt in his heart, but believes that what he says will come to pass, it will be done for him.

[5] Exodus 15:11 "Who is like you, O LORD, among the gods? Who is like you, majestic in holiness, awesome in glorious deeds, doing wonders?

[6] Psalms 29:4 The voice of the LORD is powerful; the voice of the LORD is full of majesty.

[7] 1 John 4:16 So we have come to know and to believe the love that God has for us. God is love, and whoever abides in love abides in God, and God abides in him.

[8] Exodus 34:6 The LORD passed before him and proclaimed, "The LORD, the LORD, a God merciful and gracious, slow to anger, and abounding in steadfast love and faithfulness,

[9] Romans 5:8 but God shows his love for us in that while we were still sinners, Christ died for us.

[10] Colossians 2:14 by canceling the record of debt that stood against us with its legal demands. This he set aside, nailing it to the cross.

¹¹1 Peter 2:24 He himself bore our sins in his body on the tree, that we might die to sin and live to righteousness. By his wounds you have been healed.

¹²Isaiah 53:4 Surely he has borne our griefs and carried our sorrows; yet we esteemed him stricken, smitten by God, and afflicted.

¹³Isaiah 54:17 no weapon that is fashioned against you shall succeed, and you shall refute every tongue that rises against you in judgment. This is the heritage of the servants of the LORD and their vindication from me, declares the LORD."

¹⁴Galatians 3:13 Christ redeemed us from the curse of the law by becoming a curse for us—for it is written, "Cursed is everyone who is hanged on a tree"

¹⁵Acts 3:6 But Peter said, "I have no silver and gold, but what I do have I give to you. In the name of Jesus Christ of Nazareth, rise up and walk!"

¹⁶Ephesians 6:12 For we do not wrestle against flesh and blood, but against the rulers, against the authorities, against the cosmic powers over this present darkness, against the spiritual forces of evil in the heavenly places.

¹⁷Romans 8:28 And we know that for those who love God all things work together for good, for those who are called according to his purpose.

¹⁸Revelation 12:11 And they have conquered him by the blood of the Lamb and by the word of their testimony, for they loved not their lives even unto death.

¹⁹James 1:4 And let steadfastness have its full effect, that you may be perfect and complete, lacking in nothing.

²⁰James 1:17 Every good gift and every perfect gift is from above, coming down from the Father of lights, with whom there is no variation or shadow due to change.

²¹Psalms 100:4 Enter his gates with thanksgiving, and his courts with praise! Give thanks to him; bless his name!

²²Philippians 4:6 do not be anxious about anything, but in everything by prayer and supplication with thanksgiving let your requests be made known to God.

²³Matthew 6:9-13 Pray then like this: "Our Father in heaven, hallowed be your name. Your kingdom come, your will be done, on earth as it is in heaven. Give us this day our daily bread, and forgive us our debts, as we also have forgiven our debtors. And lead us not into temptation, but deliver us from evil.

²⁴Psalms 100:4 Enter his gates with thanksgiving, and his courts with praise! Give thanks to him; bless his name!

²⁵Philippians 4:6 do not be anxious about anything, but in everything by prayer and supplication with thanksgiving let your requests be made known to God.

²⁶Psalms 37:25 I have been young, and now am old, yet I have not seen the righteous forsaken or his children begging for bread.

²⁷Deuteronomy 28:5 Blessed shall be your basket and your kneading bowl.

²⁸MarjorieLou.com/my-favorite-weapons

²⁹Jeremiah 1:12 Then the LORD said to me, "You have seen well, for I am watching over my word to perform it."

[30] 1 Corinthians 2:2 For I decided to know nothing among you except Jesus Christ and him crucified.

Chapter 12

Powerful Christians Live It Out

You have learned a lot about the power of God, its source, its immeasurable greatness, and how God puts it to work. You have begun to work out at secret power stations, building strength in God's Word, understanding of His Kingdom, and skill in handling His sword. You now know seven secrets that many pastors do not know about the power of God and how to walk in it, and you are clear as to why God's power in your life is imperative.

Your life changes right now! In your hands are all the tools to get you started as a powerful Christian. It will take practice and you must exercise perseverance as you tenaciously move forward fulfilling your Kingdom purpose life. Don't give up! Don't look back! Keep your eyes squarely on Jesus Christ as you strive to enter the rest found only in Him. The more you walk out what you have learned in this book, the easier it will become, and the more restful your life will be. Soon you will be renewed into the image of your creator, Jesus Christ.

The Purpose Behind It All

You can learn to walk in all the power God has to offer, but it will be of no avail to you unless you use it for the purpose it was intended. It is time to learn the most important, most powerful aspect of your Kingdom Life. The purpose of the power is the key to unlocking the deepest levels of power, and it reveals the deeper meaning of your Bible. This chapter will equip you to finally receive the promise of Jesus Christ that you can do all things through Him.

Power of Love

Do you remember our discussion of the Kingdom form of government in the chapter ten on authority? In such a government structure, there is one authority that exceeds all other authority. In the Kingdom of God, it is God Himself who is the Most High, most exalted One. Look what scripture tells us about our King:

...God is love.

1 John 4:8

I know you have heard this before, perhaps even way back in your childhood. But I want you to take a closer look at this statement. When this verse states God is love, it reveals the substance of Who God is. Love is what He is.

You can also say God is holy, but holy does not tell you who He is. Holy is a word that describes a quality or characteristic of God, but it does not tell you Who He is. We also know God is righteous, and God is pure. These again are attributes of God, but do not tell you Who He is. They only describe something about Him.

Love, however, tells you Who He is. Love is the substance of His being. If you are love, then holiness is a result of being love. In the same manner, righteousness is a result of being love, and purity is a result of being love. Love is not a *result* of Who He is, love *is* Who He is.

One can be loving. That would be an attribute. But to be love is itself the substance. We humans think of substance as being of a physical nature, like a list of ingredients in our favorite foods. Yet God is spirit, so His substance is not going to be three-dimensionally tangible to humans. Please take a moment to let this sink in, as it is outside our normal three-dimensional thinking. We must remember the lessons we learned in earlier chapters where we learned to think beyond our own perception and were able to take a peek behind the supernatural veil (for instance, when we talked about Elisha and His servant facing the Syrian army).

Then God said, "Let us make man in our image

Genesis 1:26

Humans are made in the image of God. Therefore, if love is the substance of Who God is, if love is what God is made up of, and we are made in the image of God, then the image we are created in is love.

We were created in the image of love. In man's perfection in the Garden of Eden before the serpent came to deceive, man was reflecting God's image. One of the awful tragedies of the fall of man in the Garden of Eden is that man no longer reflected the image of God. Man no longer reflected love. When the promised seed, Jesus Christ, finally arrived, one of the many accomplishments in His death and resurrection was restoring that ability to reflect God's image once again. We could again reflect love.

Now, if our King and highest authority is God, then understand that the authority that governs all that immeasurable greatness of power is love. This will help you understand why God makes this unusual yet remarkable statement.

> *If I speak in the tongues of men and of angels,*
> *but have not love,*
> *I am a noisy gong or a clanging cymbal.*
> *And if I have prophetic powers,*
> *and understand all mysteries*
> *and all knowledge,*
> *and if I have all faith, so as to remove mountains,*
> *but have not love,*
> *I am nothing.*
> *If I give away all I have,*
> *and if I deliver up my body to be burned,*
> *but have not love,*
> *I gain nothing.*
>
> 1 Corinthians 13:1-3

Everything you do in the name of Jesus Christ must be done by His nature. Anything God leads you to do, anything that is God's will for your life, He intends you to do according to His image. Everything the Bible tells you to do, must be done in love. Anything you do according to God's will can only be done in love, because that is Who He is. This is His will, that you do everything in love. If you do anything outside of love, it is not God's work.

Not everyone who says to me, 'Lord, Lord,' will enter the kingdom of heaven, but the one who does the will of my Father who is in heaven. On that day many will say to me, 'Lord, Lord, did we not prophesy in your name, and cast out demons in your name, and do many mighty works in your name?' And then will I declare to them, '
I never knew you;
depart from me, you workers of lawlessness.'

Matthew 7:21-23

According to Hebrews,[1] Jesus is the exact imprint of God's nature. Jesus is the exact replication of love. In other words, Jesus is a physical manifestation of the love that God is. So everything done in His name must be done in love. In the above passage we see people who view themselves as believers and who are doing amazing things in Jesus name. From Jesus' view, these people are not His at all. He calls them "workers of lawlessness." They are doing works that Jesus commands believers to do in the Great Commission as recorded in Mark 16. But if they are not done in love, it profits them absolutely nothing. "Depart from me" are not words you want to hear from Jesus when you finally stand before Him.

This is why the scriptures say if I speak in tongues but have no love, I am just a bunch of racket. If I see someone with prophetic powers, I might consider them to be very mature Christians to be able to do that. God is not impressed with outward behavior. If it is not done in love, it is worthless. If I meet a Christian who cast mountains with their great level of faith, I will be greatly impressed. God says without love, that person is nothing. Even if you are martyred for Jesus Christ, but it was not done in love, you gain nothing. Strong words. Strong message.

As we continue with the scripture from 1 Corinthians 13, Paul goes on to give a description of love. You may find it very familiar. I hope with this reading of it, you will see deeper into the purpose of it.

> *Love is patient and kind;*
> *love does not envy or boast;*
> *it is not arrogant or rude.*
> *It does not insist on its own way;*
> *it is not irritable or resentful;*
> *it does not rejoice at wrongdoing,*
> *but rejoices with the truth.*
> *Love bears all things,*
> *believes all things,*
> *hopes all things,*
> *endures all things.*
> *Love never ends*
>
> 1 Corinthians 13:4-8

The word love is so misunderstood in American society. Hollywood has polluted its meaning by representing love as selfish lust with uncontrolled passion. I see Satan's hand all over this twisting and perverting of a word that is the very exact word telling us Who God is. Satan wants to keep people from seeing truth, and his scheme against this word love goes undetected by those who do not have the Spirit of Christ to direct them.

Take the picture you have in your mind of what the word love means. Now, set it up on a shelf in the back of your mind and listen to what Paul says love is. It becomes obvious Paul is not talking about self-serving desires, nor is he referring to mushy-gushy feelings. Paul describes self-sacrificing actions and attitudes toward other people.

Love is patient, and kind
Love does not envy, or boast
Love is not arrogant, or rude
Love does not insist on its own way
Love is not irritable, or resentful
Love does not rejoice at wrongdoing, but rejoices with the truth.
Love bears all things, believes all things, hopes all things, endures all things.

One version says love hardly even notices when others do it wrong. Another version says Love doesn't keep score of the sins of others.

This is our definition of love. This is our model of love. With our new Biblical understanding of love, go back to scriptures with me.

Jesus said:

> *A new commandment I give to you,*
> *that you love one another:*
> *just as I have loved you,*
> *you also are to love one another.*
>
> *John 13:34*

Peter said:

> *...love one another earnestly from a pure heart,*
>
> *1 Peter 1:22*

John said:

> *Whoever says he is in the light and hates his brother*
> *is still in darkness.*
> *Whoever loves his brother abides in the light,*
> *and in him there is no cause for stumbling.*
> *But whoever hates his brother is in the darkness*
> *and walks in the darkness,*
> *and does not know where he is going,*
> *because the darkness has blinded his eyes.*
>
> *1 John 2:9-11*

I hope these scriptures are looking a little different to you now. When you understand the Biblical word love, these passages take on a deeper, more challenging meaning.

Paul had the most to say. He shows us in Romans 14:15, if you cause your brother to stumble by what you do (even if you are totally right) then you are no longer walking in love. His warning continues as he admonishes, by your actions do not destroy the one for whom Christ died.

Paul continues this thinking in other passages:

> Do not quarrel over opinions
> Romans 14:1
>
> Please your neighbor for his own good
> Romans 15:2
>
> Build each other up
> 1 Thessalonians 5:11

Esteem others higher than yourself
Philippians 2:3

Love is a fruit of the Holy Spirit
Galatians 5:22

Do you remember the challenge Paul gave the believers in the city of Corinth? We discussed it in Chapter 8 in relation to words you speak. Paul admonished believers for suing one another instead of settling their differences within the body of Christ. He asks them:

> *but brother goes to law against brother,*
> *and that before unbelievers?*
> *To have lawsuits at all with one another*
> *is already a defeat for you.*
> *Why not rather suffer wrong?*
> *Why not rather be defrauded?*
>
> *1 Corinthians 6:6-7*

Paul is asking these believers why they are responding like this when they are mistreated. Is it really such a big deal? Why can't you just let it go. It is, after all, what Jesus commanded us to do. Remember, "Do good to those who mistreat you." Not, "Sue the pants off them and get what's fair."

A Look in the Mirror

I ask you now to consider what you do when someone is rude to you. How do you respond if someone cheats you? If someone treats you harshly, do you immediately think of how *you* feel because of their actions? Or are you concerned for *them* and what difficulties might be in their life causing them to act so belligerent? Analyzing your response will aid you in determining whether you are being led by God's Spirit or your old selfish nature.

Paul taught us that our old nature is crucified. Crucifixion is an instrument of death. That means our old nature is dead, with all its desires and passions.[2] The desire to prove yourself right is dead. The passion to get your fair share is dead. When my old nature is crucified, I can make the same claim as Paul: I no longer live (my passions and desires) but Christ lives in me (His passions and desires).[3] Christ lives in me and the substance of the One Who lives in me is love.

Now when someone cheats me, I do good to them in return. If they curse me (telling lies about me, wishing horrible things would happen to me, or slandering me), I return words of blessing.

> *But I say to you who hear,*
> *Love your enemies,*
> *do good to those who hate you,*
> *bless those who curse you,*
> *pray for those who abuse you.*
> *To one who strikes you on the cheek, offer the other also,*
> *and from one who takes away your cloak*
> *do not withhold your tunic either.*
> *Give to everyone who begs from you,*
> *and from one who takes away your goods*
> *do not demand them back.*
> *And as you wish that others would do to you, do so to them.*
>
> Luke 6:27-31

The beatitudes, as this passage of scripture is often referred to, are not hard. They only seem hard because they go against the grain of our human nature and what the world has taught us. Once we let that old nature die and are raised into the new abundant life of Jesus Christ, living in love, we finally enter into His rest and are set free to fulfill the work of the Kingdom in just the way Jesus taught us to do it.

God wants you to walk by His nature of love, so that you can lavish that love on your spouse, your children or grandchildren, your co-worker, or your neighbors. All of the law and all of the prophets are fulfilled in love.[4] He is not asking if the people are loveable, He is commanding you to love even the most unlovable. When you do, doors open in the supernatural to pierce the hearts of contemptible humans, making the way for salvation possible.

Let me remind you once again. The Holy Spirit always leads you to walk in love, true Biblical love. Without exception, He leads you to lay down your own life. This means sacrificing your own wants, needs, desires and passions for the wants and needs of others. When you do, the deepest levels of power and understanding of God are released in your life and you will be a very powerful Christian.

When you sell out for Jesus, everything in your life will change. It is like opening floodgates of power, and through it all the hosts of heaven are released to work on your behalf. All of God's promises and protection begin to manifest. Your marriage will change, even if your spouse doesn't understand. Children in your home will respond, because they will detect the difference in your attitude and the peace in your soul. There will always be people who are upset with you, but their rampages will no longer have power over you. You will be protected under the wing of Almighty God, since your ear is bent only to Him, and you concern yourself with His opinion and no one else's.

Satan does not want you to understand what you have just read. It will depower all his best tricks against you. Do you need to go back and read this chapter again? Please do! I encourage you to read it as many times as it takes for you to see the critical importance of walking in love.

There is one final step for you to take to become a Christian that walks in God's power and lives a life of miracles and answered prayers. It presents itself in the form of a decision placed before you.

ENDNOTES

[1]Hebrews 1:3 He is the radiance of the glory of God and the exact imprint of his nature, and he upholds the universe by the word of his power. After making purification for sins, he sat down at the right hand of the Majesty on high,

[2]Romans 6:6 We know that our old self was crucified with him in order that the body of sin might be brought to nothing, so that we would no longer be enslaved to sin.

[3]Galatians 2:20 I have been crucified with Christ. It is no longer I who live, but Christ who lives in me. And the life I now live in the flesh I live by faith in the Son of God, who loved me and gave himself for me.

[4]Matthew 22:37-40 And he said to him, "You shall love the Lord your God with all your heart and with all your soul and with all your mind. This is the great and first commandment. And a second is like it: You shall love your neighbor as yourself. On these two commandments depend all the Law and the Prophets."

Chapter 13

The Valley of Decision

The modern church has awoken from her recent slumber. She realizes her power has been stripped by complacency and apathy. In response, God is calling forth believers to stand up and take hold of the immeasurable greatness of power He makes available to those who believe. He is restoring the purpose of His Kingdom through a remnant of sold out soldiers of the cross. The voice of the Father rings through the atmosphere as the Holy Spirit gently stirs your soul to listen and respond to the call.

Christians across this country are rising up for the cause of Jesus Christ. They are finding God's power and protection for their life and their family as they bring change where ever they go. Their family members share bonded hearts. Their marriages grow strong. Their children withstand the temptations of the world and are an influence in their generation for righteousness sake. They live a life of miracles and know how to pray effectively in the fullness of God's power.

This will be your life story. You can enjoy the peace of God over your family as you become a witness to your sphere of influence in this world. Accomplishing the work of the Kingdom will become your greatest joy as you serve Jesus

Christ together with your family, taking the gospel to the world and laying hands on the sick for recovery. You will stave off Satan's attacks against your household, no longer deceived by his trickery.

The power of God is now at your fingertips. With it you enjoy the protection, provision, shelter and rescue that God offers to those who dwell in the shelter of the Most High God.[1] The freedom promised in Jesus Christ will be yours and "Victory in Christ" will be your cry.

The wall that separates you from this victory is a battle raging in your mind. Everything I described about the Holy Spirit leading you to lay down your life seems too hard. Maybe you could do it for some nice people, but for that big mouth jerk that lives down the street? No way! If I am nice to him, he with think I am weak and he will get worse than ever!

Thus says the world, and therein lies your decision. In our society, a Kingdom response to nasty people is considered weakness. But in Truth, a Kingdom response is a mark of Godliness, strength and wisdom, and creates opportunities behind the veil where God can penetrate the heart of the lost. You must choose between the natural and the supernatural, the world's way or God's way. You will live like Elisha's servant, trembling before impossible situations, or you will live like Elisha, with a host of heaven released to work powerfully on your behalf. You will battle with flesh and blood, or you will wield God's sword in battle against principalities of the air. It is the decision of a lifetime. It is a decision between life and death.

You face the moment of decision. You stand at a fork in your path and you must choose your way. Will you walk the big wide path that everyone else is on? You will have a lot of company there, but they are all miserable and powerless. And so will you be. The wide path may look easier at this moment, but that is deception because it leads to destruction. You know, because your life is already a mess as you live by the world's rules. The narrow way is the way of the Kingdom that leads to life and few there be that find it.[2] Life or death. Again, the choice is yours.

Jesus said it will take a bit of struggling to enter into that narrow path, but inside you enjoy the freedom and power of your Savior and King, Christ Jesus. He said, "Take my yoke for it is easy and my burden for it is light."[3] Live my way. Walk like my Father. And you will find rest for your souls.

In Greek context, the words translated burden or heavy laden infers working to a point of exhaustion. I assure you that to scrap, fight, set others straight, prove how right you are, walk in anger and live in hate is an exhausting work. It sucks all the life out of you.

Take another look at that fork in your path. Then choose the narrow way. The few that choose that path enjoy the benefits of a life in God's power and victory in Christ.

It took me decades to discover what I have shown you in the pages of this book. I wasted years of my life frustrated that I could not seem to live as the Bible taught, even though I tried hard and desired to do what was right. The struggles were relentless as I trudged through the world chained to an enemy who toyed with me like a cat with a mouse. No more! I have been set free in Jesus Christ! My hand is to the plow and I will never look back!

Do not spend one more minute of your life struggling with every scheme the devil throws at you. Tell your emotions there is a new master over your life and His name is Jesus Christ. God has made His power available to you, so you and your family can enjoy the provision and protection He promises. Take hold of the immeasurable greatness of His power and let it work in you, transforming you and your family.

The ball is now in your court. You will finish reading this book and say, "That was nice," like the 95% who do nothing. or you will be one of the 5% who put this information into practice, get serious about the Word, and experience the immeasurable greatness of God's power.

God is calling for an army of believers who will rise up and take back their marriages, their parenting and their workplace for the cause of Jesus Christ. I have enlisted in this army to serve my King and obey His Word. He has issued me a weapon, forged by his very mouth, powerful to slay evil, overcome temptations, and stop attacks against my household. There is nothing in this world I would trade for that weapon I hold. Nothing will pry me out of the hand of my Savior. Nothing will stop me from hearing Jesus say to me,

"Well done good and faithful servant.
Enter into the joy of your master!"

Matthew 25:21

My decision is made. My family and I experience the provision and protection of God's power every day. Now you must decide. Join me, and together we will do amazing things for our King!

****

If your heart's cry is, "Yes! Lord, here I am! Use me! Teach me! I want to do amazing things for you!", then I want to help you begin walking in God's power by offering you these resources.

FREE EBOOK

I have assembled a collection of my favorite battle scriptures into an eBook entitled *My Favorite Weapons* that I'm giving you for free. Get yours now at:

MarjorieLou.com/my-favorite-weapons

FREE EBOOKLET - 7 SECRETS LIST

This eBooklet is designed for easy review and quick reference of the 7 secrets, to assist you in working out at your power stations without having to go back through the whole book. Download to your favorite device or print for free! Go to:

MarjorieLou.com/7-secrets-list

FREE PRINTABLE ARMY ENLISTMENT COMMITMENT

What better way to commemorate your enlistment into the Lord's army than to download a commitment between yourself and God. I have mine in a frame on the wall. When I face tough times and feel like giving up, I go back to read it and remember the commitment I made to God, and His promise to me that He will get me through. (Don't worry – it is only between you and God. You are not committing to anything with Marjorie Lou Ministries.) You can download it for free at:

MarjorieLou.com/army-commitment

FREE AUDIOBOOK

Don't forget! Marjorie wants to bless you with the Audio Book Edition

100% FREE!

To download go to:

MarjorieLou.com/powerful-Christian-audiobook

HERE'S WHAT YOU DO NEXT!

Bring Marjorie into YOUR home!

Online Video Course - How to Prepare Your Home for the Power of God, entitled *Welcome to Our Home, God*

MarjorieLou.com/welcome-to-our-home-God

8 video sessions and printable worksheets

Why did I make this online course? Many people told me they wished I could come to their house, sit on their couch, and help them know what to do in their own homes so they can walk in the power of God. I personally would love to come to your home, and everyone else's too! But I am physically constrained for obvious reasons. This eCourse is the next best thing!

I come into your home via 8 videos with accompanying worksheets and other bonuses throughout. I personally help you prepare your household for the power of God to flow in your home, your family, and your life. I help you educate your family members. I assist you in exposing hindrances and traps the enemy may have set for you. I give you direction in moving forward and walking in that immeasurable greatness of power God promises to those who believe.

Here is what one student had to say:

What a WEALTH of encouraging, empowering, and IMPACTFUL information. Sooo very good! Thank you for obeying God and equipping us to do the same!!!   Debbie P.

Once you buy the Course, you have access to it for LIFE! Watch it over and over again with your family!

Regular price $59.
Your discounted price ONLY $29!
That's 50% off!

Register for your Course now by going to:

MarjorieLou.com/welcome-to-our-home-God

Think of three people you know need to read this book. Then choose one of the following for each:

- Lend them your copy of the book
- Buy them a copy in their favorite format (print, eBook or audio)
  - Great gift idea!
- Send them the link to buy it for themselves

If you enjoyed this book, PLEASE LEAVE A REVIEW ON AMAZON. Marjorie loves to hear your feedback and it helps others know this book is worthy of attention!

Follow Marjorie Lou

KingdomPurposeLife.com
Facebook   @kingdompurposelife
Twitter   @marjorie_lou_

ENDNOTES

[1]Psalms 91:1 He who dwells in the shelter of the Most High will abide in the shadow of the Almighty.

[2]Matthew 7:13-14 "Enter by the narrow gate. For the gate is wide and the way is easy that leads to destruction, and those who enter by it are many. For the gate is narrow and the way is hard that leads to life, and those who find it are few.

[3]Matthew 11:30 For my yoke is easy, and my burden is light."

Be Encouraged in the Word!

Join a Community of Believers!

See the latest posts, audios and testimonies!

Just a click away!

KingdomPurposeLife.com

Facebook Page:

@kingdompurposelife

Twitter:

@marjorie_lou_

Invite Marjorie Lou to speak at your

- Conference
- Seminar
- Church
- Event

Learn more at

MarjorieLou.com

See a full list of resources from

Marjorie Lou

and Marjorie Lou Ministries

MarjorieLou.com

Facebook:

@marjorielouministries

Twitter:

@Marjorie_Lou_

www.ingramcontent.com/pod-product-compliance
Lightning Source LLC
Chambersburg PA
CBHW060042230426
43661CB00004B/622